Early Warning Systems for Financial Crises

Early Warning Systems for Financial Crises

Applications to East Asia

Edited by

Asian Development Bank

palgrave macmillan

First published 2005 by
PALGRAVE MACMILLAN
Houndmills, Basingstoke, Hampshire RG21 6XS and
175 Fifth Avenue, New York, N. Y. 10010
Companies and representatives throughout the world

PALGRAVE MACMILLAN is the global academic imprint of the Palgrave Macmillan division of St. Martin's Press, LLC and of Palgrave Macmillan Ltd. Macmillan® is a registered trademark in the United States, United Kingdom and other countries. Palgrave is a registered trademark in the European Union and other countries.

ISBN 1–4039–4938–7

This book is printed on paper suitable for recycling and made from fully managed and sustained forest sources.

A catalogue record for this book is available from the British Library.

A catalogue record for this book is available from the Library of Congress.

10 9 8 7 6 5 4 3 2 1
14 13 12 11 10 09 08 07 06 05

Printed and bound in Great Britain by
Antony Rowe Ltd, Chippenham and Eastbourne

Contents

CHAPTER 5

A Parametric EWS Model of Currency Crises for East Asia 123

by Younghoon Koo, Chang Seok Oh, Hyunsoo Joo, Seungjae Lee, and Jose Antonio Tan III

Tables and Figures

Tables

Figures

Foreword

Since the 1997 Asian financial crisis, the ASEAN+3 countries have implemented several important initiatives to strengthen regional monetary and financial cooperation, with a view to maintaining regional financial stability, supporting sustained growth, and reducing poverty. These initiatives fall into three broad areas: information exchange and policy dialogue; reserve sharing and pooling; and bond market development. In each of these areas substantive progress has been made.

Among the initiatives to strengthen policy dialogue, an important effort is to develop early warning system (EWS) models of financial crises. EWS models provide a useful framework for studying crisis events and the factors that lead up to them. While much of the academic work focuses on attempts to predict crises, policymakers are more interested in having a tool that can alert them to emerging economic and financial vulnerabilities so they can initiate appropriate policy responses in a timely manner.

To support this regional effort, in 2001 the Asian Development Bank (ADB) approved a technical assistance (TA) for an ASEAN+3 Framework for the Development of Early Warning Systems. The purpose of the TA was to develop EWS models for currency and banking crises that could be used as prototypes by the ASEAN+3 countries. ADB's Regional Economic Monitoring Unit is publishing the background papers and case studies commissioned under the TA in this book.

In implementing the TA, ADB organized two regional workshops to discuss these papers and case studies, the first in Thailand in December 2001, jointly with the Bank of Thailand and ASEAN Secretariat, and the second in the People's Republic of China in December 2002, jointly with the People's Bank of China and ASEAN Secretariat. We are grateful to all ASEAN+3 ministry of finance and central bank officials who participated in these workshops and provided comments.

We hope that this book will be of value for a wide spectrum of readers specializing in economic and financial monitoring, crisis prevention, financial risk management, macroeconomics, and international finance, both within and outside the region.

Yoshihiro Iwasaki
Head
Regional Economic Monitoring Unit

Acknowledgments

The collection of papers and case studies in this book was prepared as part of an Asian Development Bank (ADB) technical assistance project, "An ASEAN+3 Framework for the Development of Early Warning Systems." Under the overall guidance of Yoshihiro Iwasaki, Head of ADB's Regional Economic Monitoring Unit (REMU), and Pradumna B. Rana, REMU Director, the project was conceptualized, supervised, and coordinated by ADB Principal Economist Juzhong Zhuang who was also economics editor of this volume. The project concept also benefited from advice and suggestions from Andrew Berg and Hali Edison of the International Monetary Fund, Morris Goldstein of the Institute of International Economics, Graciela L. Kaminsky of George Washington University, Wenda Zhang of Manchester Metropolitan University, and officials of the ministries of finance and central banks of ASEAN+3 who participated in two regional project workshops, the first held in Thailand in 2001 and the second in the People's Republic of China in 2002. Wilhelmina Paz, Lea R. Sumulong, Roselle Dime, Richard Supangan, and Ferdinand O. Sia provided technical and research assistance. Guy Sacerdoti and Graham Dwyer copyedited the text, tables, and figures. Segundo P. dela Cruz, Jr. typeset the book and conceptualized its design. Ma. Rosario J. Razon and Lilibeth Perez provided secretarial support. Finally, the views expressed in this book are those of the authors and do not necessarily reflect the views and policies of the Asian Development Bank, or its Board of Governors or the governments they represent. The Asian Development Bank does not guarantee the accuracy of the data included in this publication and accepts no responsibility for any consequences of their use.

Contributors

Stijn Claessens
Professor of International Finance
University of Amsterdam
Netherlands

Morris Goldstein
Dennis Weatherstone Senior Fellow
Institute for International Economics
United States

Hyunsoo Joo
Strategist
Tong Yang Investment Bank
Republic of Korea

Younghoon Koo
Managing Director
Lotte Economic Research Center
Republic of Korea

Seungjae Lee
Research Analyst
Early Warning System Team
Korea Center for International Finance
Republic of Korea

Chang Seok Oh
Chief Strategist, Head
Early Warning System Team
Korea Center for International Finance
Republic of Korea

Pradumna B. Rana
Director
Regional Economic Monitoring Unit
Asian Development Bank
Philippines

Jose Antonio Tan III
Consultant
Asian Development Bank
Philippines

Juzhong Zhuang
Principal Economist
Asian Development Bank
Philippines

Abbreviations

ADB	Asian Development Bank
ASEAN	Association of Southeast Asian Nations (Brunei Darussalam, Cambodia, Indonesia, Lao People's Democratic Republic, Malaysia, Myanmar, Philippines, Singapore, Thailand, and Viet Nam)
ASEAN+3	ASEAN, People's Republic of China, Japan, and Republic of Korea
BI	Bank Indonesia
BIS	Bank for International Settlements
BNM	Bank Negara Malaysia
BOK	Bank of Korea
BOT	Bank of Thailand
BSP	Bangko Sentral ng Pilipinas
CAMEL	capital adequacy, asset quality, management soundness, earnings, and liquidity
CAMELS	capital adequacy, asset quality, management soundness, earnings, liquidity, and sensitivity to market risk
CPI	consumer price index
CVI	contagion vulnerability index
DCSD	Developing Country Studies Division
EWS	early warning system
FDI	foreign direct investment
FSI	financial soundness indicator
GDF	Global Development Finance
GDI	gross domestic investment
GDP	gross domestic product
GKR	Goldstein, Kaminsky, and Reinhart
HP	Hodrick-Prescott
IFS	International Financial Statistics
IIF	Institute of International Finance
IMF	International Monetary Fund
KCIF	Korea Center for International Finance

LSDV	least squares dummy variable
MAS	Monetary Authority of Singapore
MTI	Ministry of Trade and Industry
NBER	National Bureau of Economic Research
NESDB	National Economic and Social Development Board
NPL	nonperforming loan
NSR	noise-to-signal ratio
REMU	Regional Economic Monitoring Unit
SEACEN	The South East Asian Central Banks
TA	technical assistance

CHAPTER 1

Overview

Juzhong Zhuang and Pradumna B. Rana

1.1 Introduction

The 1997 Asian financial crisis showed that inconsistent macroeconomic policies can imperil the safety of financial systems, and that weak financial systems can also easily undermine macroeconomic fundamentals. With increasing globalization and international capital flows, vulnerabilities in one economy can quickly spill over to affect others. Wise policy choices and institutional reforms not only benefit a country itself, but also benefit neighbors with closely tied economies. Consequently, there has been heightened interest since the crisis in strengthening economic and financial risk management at national, regional, and international levels. Improved risk management mechanisms within and among countries, including information exchange, regional economic monitoring, and policy dialogue, are increasingly being recognized as vital for maintaining domestic, regional, and global economic and financial stability.

Among many initiatives, one that is attracting the attention of governments, multilateral institutions, investment houses, and academics is early warning systems (EWS) that could signal approaching financial crises. EWS models provide a useful framework to systematically study crisis events and associated factors. In the past few years, attempts to develop EWS models have received new impetus from the work of Kaminsky, Lizondo, and Reinhart (1998); Kaminsky and Reinhart (1999); Berg and Pattillo (1999); Goldstein, Kaminsky, and Reinhart (2000); and Edison (2000), some supported by the International Monetary Fund (IMF). While much of the academic work on

EWS focuses on trying to predict crises, policymakers are more interested in having a tool that can alert them to accumulated economic and financial weaknesses or vulnerabilities, thus enabling them to make appropriate policy responses.

To assist ASEAN+3[1] strengthen its capacity for economic monitoring, the Asian Development Bank (ADB) approved technical assistance (TA) for an ASEAN+3 Framework for the Development of Early Warning Systems in 2001. The main objective of the TA was to support ASEAN+3 collaborative efforts to develop EWS models that would help detect emerging macroeconomic, financial, and corporate sector vulnerabilities in an attempt to prevent future financial crises. Several background papers and case studies were commissioned under the TA to look into the feasibility of developing EWS models of currency and banking crises that could be used as prototypes by ASEAN+3 countries. This book presents the background papers and case studies.

1.2 Key Findings

In Chapter 2, Stijn Claessens provides a literature survey of currency and banking crisis theories. In the case of currency crises, key ingredients of three generations of theoretical models are presented. The first generation models view currency crises as the result of weak economic fundamentals. The second generation models show that currency crises can occur due to certain government policy actions, self-fulfilling expectations of market participants, and the possibility of multiple equilibriums, even in the absence of fundamental weaknesses. The third generation models, which emerged largely after the 1997 Asian financial crisis, view a currency crisis as a financial panic or run on an economy.

In the case of banking crises, much of the theory focuses on special characteristics of banks—such as maturity and currency transformation, and asymmetric information. These make banks and the banking industry vulnerable to runs and collapses following adverse shocks of either domestic or external origin. A single bank run can by contagion lead to a systemic banking crisis. Institutional features of economies, such as excessive deposit insurance, poor supervision, and weak corporate governance, are emphasized

[1] ASEAN+3 consists of the 10 members of the Association of Southeast Asian Nations (Brunei Darussalam, Cambodia, Indonesia, Lao People's Democratic Republic, Malaysia, Myanmar, Philippines, Singapore, Thailand, and Viet Nam) plus People's Republic of China, Japan, and Republic of Korea.

in the literature—as these are closely related to the incentives of bank managers to take on risks in lending operations.

In Chapter 3, Morris Goldstein reviews recent progress in developing and applying EWS models for banking and currency crises in emerging economies. The review starts with broad guidelines for conducting an early warning exercise. These include looking beyond the last prominent crisis (or group of crises) to a large sample; paying as much attention to banking crises as to currency crises; selecting data frequency in line with the purposes of the exercise; making use of a relatively wider array of early warning indicators; and employing out-of-sample tests to help gauge the usefulness of "leading indicators."

The review then discusses several key methodological issues, including how to define currency and banking crises, how to define the "early" in early warning, how to select leading indicators, and how to identify the best leading indicators and to estimate crisis probabilities. This discussion is followed by a summary of representative findings from early warning literature. A key message from these findings is that banking crises and currency crises in emerging markets do not typically arrive without any warning, and that there are recurring behavior patterns in the period leading up to them. Finally, several promising extensions are suggested to improve the performance of EWS models.

In Chapter 4, Juzhong Zhuang presents key findings of one of the two case studies of the TA—nonparametric EWS models of currency and banking crises for East Asia. The study involves estimating a currency crisis EWS model and a banking crisis EWS model following the signaling approach pioneered by Kaminsky and Reinhart (1999). The models differ from existing studies in that they focus on monthly data of a smaller but more homogeneous set of countries—Indonesia, Republic of Korea (Korea), Malaysia, Philippines, Singapore, and Thailand—and they attempt to make several methodological improvements. The chapter shows that the two EWS models have reasonably good predictive power, especially compared with most EWS models reported in other studies.

The currency crisis EWS model defines a currency crisis as an episode of monthly depreciation of a domestic currency against the US dollar exceeding the sample mean by two standard deviations. Using 1970–1995 as the sample period, the model identifies 28 currency crisis episodes and selects 40 leading indicators out of more than 60 macroeconomic and financial indicators screened as predictors of these crisis episodes. The top 9 leading indicators are found to be at least twice as likely to issue early warning signals within a "crisis window" (defined as 24 months prior to a crisis) as they are outside a crisis window. These are

- deviation of the real exchange rate against the US dollar from its trend,
- ratio of short-term external debt to foreign reserves,
- ratio of deposits in Bank for International Settlements (BIS) banks to foreign reserves,
- ratio of broad money (M2) to foreign reserves,
- 12-month change in the ratio of short-term capital flows to gross domestic product (GDP),
- ratio of foreign liabilities to foreign assets of the banking sector,
- 12-month change in the ratio of short-term external debt to foreign reserves,
- ratio of current account balance to gross domestic investment (GDI), and
- 12-month percentage change in real commercial bank deposits.

Two general and six sector-specific composite indexes—current account, capital account, financial sector, real sector, fiscal sector, and global economy—are constructed based on the 40 leading indicators. The composite indexes are found to be able to predict three quarters of the currency crisis episodes during the 1970–1995 sample period with a reasonable level of accuracy and lead time. Applying the currency crisis EWS model to 1996 and 1997 data as an out-of-sample test, it is found that the model is able to predict the 1997 currency crisis episodes in at least four of the five crisis-affected countries—Indonesia, Korea, Malaysia, Philippines, and Thailand—at a cutoff probability of 60%. The model issues persistent warning signals starting as early as 20 months prior to the 1997 crisis for Malaysia, Philippines, and Thailand.

Using banking crisis episodes documented by Goldstein, Kaminsky, and Reinhart (2000)—where the beginning of a banking crisis was marked by bank runs; or closures, mergers, or takeovers of important financial institutions; or large-scale government assistance to the banking sector—the banking crisis EWS model selects 40 leading indicators from the same set of macroeconomic and financial indicators as the currency crisis model. Nineteen of the 40 selected leading indicators are found to be at least twice as likely to issue early warning signals within a crisis window as they are outside a crisis window. The top 10 leading indicators are

- ratio of foreign liabilities to foreign assets of the banking sector,
- months of imports covered by foreign reserves,
- US real interest rate,
- ratio of short-term external debt to foreign reserves,
- 12-month change in the domestic real interest rate,
- 12-month change in the ratio of short-term capital flows to GDP,

- ratio of deposits in BIS banks to foreign reserves,
- level of world oil prices in US dollars,
- ratio of net credit to the public sector to GDP, and
- 12-month change in the ratio of short-term external debt to foreign reserves.

Two general and six sector-specific composite indexes are also constructed on the basis of the 40 leading indicators. With a reasonable level of accuracy and lead time, the model is able to predict most of the eight banking crisis episodes during the 1970–1995 in-sample period. The out-of-sample test shows that the 1997 banking crisis episodes in the Philippines and Thailand are predicted by the general composite indexes at a cutoff probability of 30%, with a lead time of 8 months. The financial sector composite index is found to issue persistent warning signals in most crisis-affected countries as early as 18 months prior to the 1997 crisis at a cutoff probability of 30%. At a cutoff probability of 50%, it still predicts the crisis in Indonesia, Korea, Philippines, and Thailand, although with less warning signals and a shorter lead time.

Chapter 4 also shows that, overall, the currency crisis model outperforms the banking crisis model. For both models, the weighted general composite index is the most reliable. Three sector-specific composite indexes also have significant predictive power: the current account and capital account indexes for the currency crisis model, and the financial sector index for the banking crisis model.

In the final chapter, Younghoon Koo, Chang Seok Oh, Hyunsoo Joo, Seungjae Lee, and Jose Antonio Tan III present findings of another case study of the TA, a parametric EWS model of currency crises for East Asia. The model is estimated using panel data and discrete choice econometric techniques. It differs from the parametric currency crisis EWS model developed by the IMF, known as the Developing Country Studies Division (DCSD) model, in that it is estimated using a smaller data set than the one used by the DCSD model, involving only six East Asian countries. It also builds on the nonparametric currency crisis EWS model described in Chapter 4 in two ways. First, it adopts the same definition of a currency crisis and has the same set of identified crisis episodes. And second, the explanatory variables are selected from the top 15 leading indicators identified by the nonparametric currency crisis EWS model.

The estimation results show that the following explanatory variables are good predictors of currency crises in the six East Asian countries during 1970–1995:

- deviation of the real exchange rate against the US dollar from its trend,
- deviation of the US dollar/yen real exchange rate from its trend,

- ratio of current account balance to GDI,
- ratio of short-term external debt to foreign reserves,
- 12-month change of the lending-deposit rate spread,
- 12-month change in the ratio of deposits in BIS banks to foreign reserves, and
- ratio of M2 to foreign reserves.

In-sample tests show that the model has good predictive power, and outperforms the IMF's DCSD model. At a cutoff probability of 30%, the model is at least 6.6 times as likely to issue early warning signals within a crisis window as it is outside a crisis window. The out-of-sample test shows that the model is capable of predicting the 1997 Asian financial crisis in at least four of the five crisis-affected countries.

1.3 Policy Implications

A key conclusion that can be drawn from these studies, which reinforces findings from earlier studies on EWS models, is that there are usually early signs in terms of a buildup of economic and financial vulnerabilities prior to an outbreak of currency or banking crises. This suggests that EWS models of the kind presented in this book could play an important role in economic monitoring and surveillance—and in policy analysis and policy making. By devising appropriate policy measures in response to early warning signals from such models, the chance of experiencing financial crises by a country or region could be reduced, if not entirely eliminated. Therefore, current efforts to develop EWS models by the ASEAN+3 countries should contribute to economic and financial stability both in these countries and in the region.

Despite the encouraging results of the studies of this TA and elsewhere, it is still too early to consider EWS models as well-established analytic tools for policy analysis and policy making. Several limitations of EWS modeling suggest that, at their current stage of development, EWS models can complement but cannot yet substitute traditional methods of economic monitoring and policy analysis; results obtained from EWS models need to be interpreted with caution and care.

First, our understanding of financial crises remains limited and, therefore, the theoretical validity of EWS models that build on the understanding of financial crises needs to be scrutinized more carefully.

Second, as emphasized in the book, there are many unresolved theoretical, empirical, and methodological issues in EWS modeling. These unresolved issues mean that EWS modeling is still at an early stage of development.

Third, the performance of EWS models in general leaves much room for improvement. Although EWS models presented in this book outperform most of those reported elsewhere, they missed many crisis episodes, and issued many false warning signals.

And finally, good performance of EWS models in sample does not guarantee equally good performance out of sample—in predicting future crisis events—because causes of financial crises have varied in the past, and could vary in the future. This is especially true with the rapid pace of structural changes and regime shifts in emerging economies partly brought about by globalization.

These limitations of EWS modeling point to the need for continued work and research by policy analysts and academics. The studies presented in this book represent such efforts.

References

Berg, Andrew, and Catherine Pattillo. 1999. Are Currency Crises Predictable: A Test. *IMF Staff Papers* 46 (2): 107–138.

Edison, Hali J. 2000. Do Indicators of Financial Crises Work? An Evaluation of an Early Warning System. *International Finance Discussion Paper No. 675*. Board of Governors of the Federal Reserve System, Washington DC, July.

Goldstein, Morris, Graciella L. Kaminsky, and Carmen M. Reinhart. 2000. *Assessing Financial Vulnerability: An Early Warning System for Emerging Markets.* Washington DC: Institute for International Economics.

Kaminsky, Graciela L., Saul Lizondo, and Carmen M. Reinhart. 1998. Leading Indicators of Currency Crises. *IMF Staff Papers* 45 (1): 1–48.

Kaminsky, Graciela L., and Carmen M. Reinhart. 1999. The Twin Crises: the Causes of Banking and Balance-of-Payments Problems. *American Economic Review* 89 (3): 473–500.

CHAPTER 2

Theories of Currency and Banking Crises: A Literature Review

Stijn Claessens

2.1 Introduction

Currency and banking crises in Latin America, Europe, and Asia over the past three decades have generated substantial literature on their causes. The literature on currency crises begins with models developed to explain crises experienced by some Latin American countries in the late 1970s. These models view currency crises as being caused by weak economic fundamentals. Following the collapse of the European Monetary System in 1992, the so-called second-generation models of currency crises emerged. These models show that currency crises can occur due to certain government policy actions, self-fulfilling expectations of market participants, and possibilities of multiple equilibriums, even in the absence of fundamental weaknesses. The theoretical currency crisis literature has expanded further since the 1997 Asian financial crisis. The so-called third-generation models view a currency crisis as a run on an economy or a financial panic.

In the case of banking crises, much of the theory focuses on special characteristics of banks—such as maturity and currency transformation, and asymmetric information—that make banks and the banking industry vulnerable to runs and collapses following adverse shocks of either domestic or external origin. A single bank run can by contagion lead to a systemic banking crisis. Institutional features of economies, such as excessive deposit insurance, poor supervision, and weak corporate governance, are emphasized in the literature as these are closely related to the incentives of bank managers to take on risks in lending operations.

The rest of this chapter reviews theories of currency and banking crises in some detail. Section 2 describes the three generations of currency crisis models. Section 3 looks at causes of banking crises. Section 4 concludes the review by outlining current thinking on how currency and (systemic) banking crises can be prevented and their impact limited.

2.2 Theory of Currency Crises

A review of the theory regarding currency crises is best done utilizing the so-called three generations of models. The first-generation models began with the seminal pieces by Krugman (1979) and Flood and Garber (1984), which were built on work by Salant and Henderson (1978). The key focus of these papers was that macro policies, defined broadly, can (i) be inconsistent when combined with fixed or pegged exchange rates, (ii) lead to an unsustainable situation, and (iii) be followed by a currency adjustment. These macro inconsistencies may include excessive domestic credit growth, fiscal weaknesses, and poor economic performance, to mention only a few. The major contribution of these papers was not so much the point that inconsistencies can lead to currency adjustments, as that is well understood. Rather, it was the prediction that there could be a sharp and sudden loss in foreign exchange reserves when forward-looking market participants realized that the existing exchange rate was no longer viable.

The first generation of currency crisis models can be interpreted more broadly. It is not only that the policy inconsistencies can be macroeconomic; they can also be of a microeconomic or other nature. The inconsistencies with a fixed or pegged foreign exchange rate can thus also be attributable to the presence of some structural weaknesses. For example, a decline in competitiveness as a result of poor labor upgrading can mean that a foreign exchange rate target is no longer viable; a weakening of export prices due to new competition can make macro policies—including the foreign exchange rate target—more inconsistent. As such, the first-generation literature on currency crises can be seen to view currency crises as fundamental-based events.

The second generation of currency crisis models began with Obstfeld (1986 and 1996; see also Krugman 1997). Obstfeld stressed that there may be trade-offs between various policy objectives pursued by a country. For example, inflation and employment may face some trade-offs, as in the traditional Phillips curve. The government may be indifferent between, say, an outcome of low inflation and high unemployment or an outcome of high inflation and low unemployment. The low inflation equilibrium may be associated with a fixed exchange rate and the high inflation outcome with a floating exchange rate regime or another fixed, but depreciated, exchange rate. If the government (or the country, more generally) is indifferent to the two outcomes, either equilibrium may be sustained, thus opening up the possibility of multiple equilibriums, and associated sudden currency adjustments.

Prospective fiscal deficits caused by a collapse of a banking system and the need for a fiscal bailout may also trigger a currency crisis—the expectation of the government having to bail out a banking system may cause lenders to pull out funds, thus triggering the collapse of the currency and creating a crisis (Burnside, Eichenbaum, and Rebelo 2001). This means that one can have self-fulfilling currency crises, that is, because of some events or actions (for example, by a speculator), the equilibrium may shift from a fixed regime to a floating regime or from one fixed exchange rate to another fixed but depreciated rate.

There are other related models. Blanchard and Watson (1982) model the collapse of a stochastic speculative bubble that was itself a rational equilibrium. The bubble, however, was nevertheless *ex post* irrational and also had a positive probability of collapsing all along. Typically, this has been applied more to stock markets. In some cases, however, the exchange rate has displayed some of the same patterns, such as in Russia in the summer of 1998 when the exchange rate and the fiscal situation were being supported by large capital inflows that all along seemed to have a large probability of collapsing.

The theoretical currency crisis literature has expanded further since the 1997 Asian financial crisis. The so-called third-generation models view a currency crisis as a run on a country or a financial panic. In some sense, the country is subject to the equivalent of a bank run with the fixed (or pegged) exchange rate functioning as the equivalent of a fixed deposit contract. As such, the literature builds on the seminal model of Diamond and Dybvig (1983) of bank runs. The first and most complete version of this analogy in the banking crisis literature is Chang and Velasco (2001).

More broadly, the third-generation models draw attention to the structure of claims on a country as it affects the risk of a financial crisis. Creditors, particularly those with short-term claims, can suddenly withdraw, leaving the country with an acute shortage of foreign exchange and liquidity. The withdrawal may be rational for each creditor given the lack of coordination among creditors—each individual's incentive is to withdraw first, fearing that others will withdraw even earlier. The effect on the country, however, is a loss of aggregate liquidity that triggers a currency or financial collapse.

Even more broadly, the third-generation models have drawn attention to the importance of balance sheet effects for the sustainability of a currency target. Papers on this topic include Krugman (1999); Caballero and Krishnamurthy (2001); and Aghion, Bachetta, and Banerjee (2000). In Krugman (1999), the argument is that balance sheet mismatches can force banks or corporations to quickly generate demand for foreign exchange. With a large part of the financial sector or corporate sector seeking foreign exchange, however, pressure is put on the foreign exchange rate. As the rate depreciates, more financial institutions or corporations may seek foreign exchange to cover open positions, stimulating even further aggregate outflows and thereby triggering a currency crisis. Caballero and Krishnamurthy (2001) point out that these events may be more likely in emerging markets because firms and banks there cannot easily collateralize their foreign exchange assets or cash flows. As such, they have less ability to smooth shocks, and a relatively small event can trigger large capital outflows and a currency crisis.

There are many variations of the basic third-generation currency crisis models, all of which center on balance sheet effects and capital market imperfections. One such theory is the disorderly workout (Sachs 1994a and 1994b; and Miller and Zhang 2000). This theory can be seen as the equivalent of a grab for assets in the absence of a domestic bankruptcy system, as in the case of a liquidity problem of a firm. Because an effective means of reorganizing claims in case of an international liquidity problem does not exist, a disorderly workout can easily result when a country is hit by a small shock that ought to be only a liquidity shock. The liquidity shock may turn into an insolvency situation, however, because the corporations and financial institutions in the country, with no access to good restructuring mechanisms, will destroy value, creating a debt overhang.

An international bankruptcy regime for sovereign claims could prevent a liquidity shock for a government from becoming a solvency issue, and there has been much research and policy discussion under way recently in this area (such as the Sovereign Debt Restructuring Mechanism; see Krueger 2002). Even when an international bankruptcy regime for sovereign claims could be introduced, the issue of restructuring remains for international claims on domestic corporations and financial institutions. For these, local insolvency regimes are often insufficient and, almost always, poorly equipped to deal with the large number of claims in a systemic crisis and the ensuing complexities of international restructuring.

Another type of currency crisis that has received attention under the third-generation models is the "moral hazard induced crisis." Excessive, overly risky investment by banks, other financial institutions, or corporations may be induced by government behavior or policy. Specifically, risky banks may be able to borrow cheaply as they have implicit or explicit guarantees from the government on their liabilities, that is, implicit or explicit deposit insurance. If they are or become undercapitalized and are weakly regulated, then the incentive for them to increase risk becomes very large. Akerlof and Romer (1993) model what they call looting behavior in the context of the US Savings and Loan Crisis in the early 1980s. This model has been extended, although not always formally, to the situation of a currency crisis. The addition is that both foreign and domestic creditors go along with the risky behavior of financial institutions or corporations, as they know that the government or international financial institutions will bail them out.

Krugman (1998) applies this model to the Asian crisis. Dooley (2000) generalizes the model with any form of government guarantee. Johnson, Boone, Breach, and Friedman (2000) apply this to cases of weak corporate governance. They show that a weak institutional framework of corporate governance can mean that controlling shareholders become more interested in looting a firm when hit by a small shock. In turn, this can trigger a currency crisis. They provide empirical support for this across several countries as the degree of currency depreciation is related to the quality of the institutional framework.

A last form of recent currency crisis models, although not necessarily belonging to the third-generation models, has been related to the phenomena of contagion in real and financial markets. It is obvious that global shocks, such as rises in interest rates or oil price changes, may affect a whole group of countries simultaneously and thus create crises on a large scale that may suggest spillovers but are really fundamental-based crises. There may also be other ways by which a crisis in one country spills over into other parts of the world. For example, these can be trade links invoking competitive devaluations. They can also be financial links related to things like foreign direct investment (FDI) where, for example, events in Thailand can trigger a crisis in Indonesia as Thai investors pull out of Indonesia. The common lender channel is one specific form of this kind of contagion. In the East Asian financial crisis, Japan was found to transmit shocks in this way, while the US played a role in Latin American crises. A crisis in one country may also teach investors something about fundamentals in other, similar countries. This is not necessarily contagion, but rather learning about the true model of risk. Following the Asian financial crisis, many observers have used the concept of a "wake-up call." In one sense, this concept and some of the other contagion models are more a part of first- or second-generation currency and banking crisis models.

Nonetheless, financial markets frequently are cited as the sole or main culprit of financial crises. As such, there may be an independent role for financial markets in causing financial crises. There are still two dimensions or situations to consider. One is when there is some rational behavior in financial markets that, nevertheless, has perverse effects. Much of this would derive from coordination issues in financial markets—individuals may act rationally on their own, but collectively they may cause a bad outcome, such as a bank run. The degree of this behavior can be affected by many institutional features, such as the prevalence of benchmarking on index portfolios among investment managers or the degree of agency issues among investment fund managers. Information asymmetries may aggravate the issue when investors follow insiders deemed to have better information. The other dimension is the truly irrational behavior at the individual level. This irrational behavior can include herding or prevalence of multiple equilibriums at the level of asset classes (for example, emerging markets may be considered "out of fashion").

The distinction between the individually rational but collectively irrational and the individually irrational is theoretically unclear and often empirically impossible to tell. Debates still rage on whether the Asian financial crisis was caused by either form. Therefore, some have argued that it is more relevant to investigate whether there are policy interventions that can affect either type of behavior. This still requires, however, a test to determine whether indeed either effect is considered to have purely negative effects. After all, some forms of "contagion" represent a normal allocation of resources and good form of market discipline. Furthermore, each policy intervention raises its own trade-offs, such as moral hazard in the case of an international lender as a last resort to counteract the individually rational but collectively irrational run on a country.

2.3 Theory of Banking Crises

There are two types of banking distress—individual bank distress and system-wide banking distress. The theory regarding causes of the first type takes a more micro view and has been applied extensively to the empirical models used mainly in developed countries to predict financial distress. Reviewing this theory is relevant here because individual banking distress can lead to systemic distress, depending upon various factors. Although the theory dealing with determinants of system-wide banking distress is somewhat similar to that regarding individual bank distress, there are some important differences and additions, several of which have already been reviewed under the theory of currency crises. A review of both types follows.

Much of the literature on bank runs has modeled the phenomenon as an asymmetric information problem between depositors and banks. Some consider these banking panics as random manifestations of mass hysteria or mob psychology, as discussed by Kindleberger (1978). This "pure panic" or "sunspot" theory of a bank run is formalized in Diamond and Dybvig (1983). They posit that illiquidity of assets provides the rationale for a bank's vulnerability to runs. Multiple equilibriums can exist where one of the equilibrium points is a bank run scenario arising from the panic of agents. They also show that a bank run can be self-fulfilling when depositors believe that other depositors are withdrawing their funds even without any initial deterioration of the bank's balance sheet.

In predicting individual bank insolvency, the empirical approach typically used in developed countries has been a combination of micro factors, summarized in the CAMEL framework—capital adequacy, asset quality, management soundness, earnings, and liquidity. Poor balance sheets (nonperforming loans, or NPLs), poor profitability, balance sheet mismatches, low liquidity, weak governance, and excessive risk-taking have been found to lead to vulnerabilities and banking distress. Because bank runs occur more often in developing countries—as market solutions to temporary liquidity problems do not work as well as in developed countries, and deposit insurance is not always credible—interbank market and other institutional structures have been important factors to consider in these countries.

Also in developing countries, shocks to interest rates, the foreign exchange rate, and stock prices, or an economic slowdown and recession can create individual bank distress. Legacies can also be important. Often a bank's inherited weak balance sheet will appear during or after financial liberalization. This is true with other reforms as well. For example, in many transition economies, pre-transition banks suffered from having to allocate resources to state-owned enterprises. These only surfaced when the corporate and banking sectors were being reformed.

The theory of banking system insolvency begins from the theory of individual bank distress. Chari and Jagannathan (1988) provide an extension of the Diamond-Dybvig model to explain banking panics. They posit that banking panics result from the misinterpretation by uninformed depositors of liquidity withdrawals as being withdrawals caused by pessimistic information on bank assets. Jacklin and Bhattacharya (1988) further distinguish between pure panics and information-based bank runs by emphasizing the source of bank runs as the role played by interim private information about bank loans and asset payoffs. Both models can be interpreted to imply that a single bank run causes a system-wide banking crisis. Another version is that bank runs systematically relate to events that change the perception of depositors' risk—such as extreme seasonal fluctuations (Miron 1985), unexpected failure of a large (typically financial) corporation, and major cyclical downturns (Gorton 1988). Mishkin (1996) provides a broader framework for the role of asymmetric information in financial crises in developing countries.

Another propagation mechanism is contagion through interbank deposits. Spillovers of individual banking distress can affect the entire banking system via interbank lending. Factors like the size of financial institutions and the functioning of interbank and other financial markets will determine the likelihood of contagion. In this respect, banks in emerging markets are more at risk. In theoretical models, Allen and Gale (2000) show that, to protect themselves against liquidity preference shocks, banks hold interbank claims with each other that are interregional in nature. However, this opens the possibility of a small liquidity preference shock in one bank or region to spread throughout the economy. Another propagation mechanism, suggested by Diamond and Rajan (2002), assumes that banks have a common pool of liquidity. Bank failures can cause aggregate liquidity shortages, which can lead to the failure of other banks, thus making a total meltdown possible even without any informational or contractual links between banks.

The micro factors that can be important determinants for banking system distress refer to the quality of a country's entire institutional framework. Poor market discipline due to moral hazard, limited disclosure, a weak corporate governance framework, excessive deposit insurance, or poor supervision can determine the degree of information asymmetries, quality of bank management, and the buildup of vulnerabilities, which in turn can trigger banking system crises.

At the system level, macroeconomic factors—shocks to interest rates, foreign exchange devaluations, commodity price shocks, economic slowdowns, and capital outflows—can also be important determinants of crises. Banking crises can be triggered by sudden capital outflows as shown by Calvo, Leiderman, and Reinhart (1994). Foreign currency exposures by banks and their subsequent issuance of foreign currency-denominated domestic loans can make banks vulnerable to external shocks (Chinn and Kletzer 2000). System-wide problems can include legacies, which become public with or after financial liberalization. Finally, there are many cases when poor early intervention drives a small degree of distress into a major banking crisis. For example, ad hoc policy approaches can cause confusion among depositors, trigger further runs, and lead to a full-scale financial crisis. These causes have been reviewed in many papers.

2.4 How to Prevent and Limit Financial Crises

Understanding currency and banking crises and their causes can help policymakers reduce the chance of their occurrence. The policy elements necessary to achieve this reduction have been much discussed in the debate over international financial architecture during the past few years. These include better macroeconomic management, such as fiscal and exchange rate management, which will help reduce the risks of unsustainable exchange rates and currency crises. Changes to the international financial system itself may help prevent liquidity crises from becoming crises in solvency. For a review of these broader design issues of the international financial architecture, refer to Fischer (2002).

The debate on international financial architecture has also led to new guidance on improving the way the financial sector functions. The elements include a drive for better regulation and supervision, although one must realize the regulatory and supervisory limits in weak institutional environments, as in many developing countries (as highlighted by Barth, Caprio, and Levine 2003). Increasing private sector mechanisms for monitoring is useful for financial sector stability and efficiency. Increasing banking system transparency by way of greater shareholdings of foreign banks and other financial institutions is one example. And it will remain important to apply some limits to bank operations, such as limits on maturity mismatches, portfolio composition, foreign exchange exposure, and asset growth.

An important but often overlooked dimension to systemic bank crises is that their output losses, and fiscal and other costs can be controlled. What has become general "best practice" advice on managing a banking crisis can limit costs—intervene early and address problems comprehensively and credibly; structure and manage recapitalizations adequately; do not close banks without alternative financial intermediation mechanisms in place; and complement bank restructuring with corporate restructuring. This "best practice" advice also involves proactive policies, such as supporting the core, good elements of the financial sector by providing financial support to healthy banks, or at least banks with intrinsic franchise value, and by having some adequately designed lender of last resort facility. Possibly some support to corporations is needed, such as help for small- and medium-sized firms in the form of working capital financing or, more generally, support for trade finance.

Many countries do not follow best practice policies, however, making small banking crises grow systemic and become very costly. Honohan and Klingebiel (2000) show that poor early crisis management can add 35–75% of the cross-country variation in fiscal costs of crises. Most costly are the provisions of open-ended liquidity support to insolvent financial institutions; the issuance of an unlimited guarantee of financial institutions' liabilities, not limited to deposits; and the policy of regulatory forbearance and repeated recapitalizations. If a country pursues best practice policies, fiscal costs of a crisis would be only 0.98% of gross domestic product (GDP), whereas with bad policies, fiscal costs would be 62.6% of GDP. Importantly, the analysis shows that the effects on economic growth of these bad policies are little or even perverse, that is, these policies hardly enhance economic growth, or perhaps even retard it. This suggests that these policies, especially the blanket guarantee, are largely government transfers—from some taxpayers to other, privileged taxpayers. As such, systemic banking crises are very much a function of the policies adopted and the political economy.

Countries should expect and be prepared for future financial crises. A vigilant monitoring of vulnerabilities and financial exposures is needed to limit both the risk of financial crises and the impact an actual crisis will have. This can take the form of frequent financial stability assessments using well-designed analytic and forecasting frameworks, including the early warning systems presented in the rest of this volume. Some degree of contingency crisis planning can also be useful, particularly on how to react to the first sign of an incipient banking crisis, as that often determines whether or not a more systemic crisis results. Most importantly, however, countries need to continually enhance their overall incentive framework so that private sector financial institutions and corporations are willing and able to manage their financial risks properly. This requires good macroeconomic management, including proper exchange rate management and ensuring that all three pillars for achieving a solid financial and corporate sector are in place: private capital for backing up financial institutions and corporations, and providing adequate incentives for risk management; an active market role in monitoring and disciplining financial institutions and corporations; and the public sector in its role of supervising financial institutions.

References

Aghion, Philippe, Philippe Bacchetta, and Abhijit Banerjee. 2000. A Simple Model of Monetary Policy and Currency Crises. *European Economic Review* 44 (4–6): 728–738.

Akerlof, George, and Paul Romer. 1993. Looting the Economic Underworld of Bankruptcy for Profit. *Brookings Papers on Economic Activity* 2:1–73.

Allen, Franklin, and Douglas Gale. 2000. Financial Contagion. *Journal of Political Economy* 108 (1): 1–33.

Barth, J. R., G. Caprio Jr., and R. Levine. 2003. Bank Supervision and Regulation: What Works Best? *Journal of Financial Intermediation*. Forthcoming.

Blanchard, Olivier, and Mark Watson. 1982. Bubbles, Rational Expectations and Financial Markets. In *Crises in the Economic and Financial Structure*, edited by Paul Wachtel. Lexington: Lexington Books.

Burnside, Craig, Martin Eichenbaum, and Sergio Rebelo. 2001. Prospective Deficits and the Asian Currency Crisis. *Journal of Political Economy* 109 (6): 1155–1197.

Caballero, Ricardo J., and Arvind Krishnamurthy. 2001. International and Domestic Collateral Constraints in a Model of Emerging Market Crises. *Journal of Monetary Economics* 48 (3): 513–548.

Calvo, G., L. Leiderman, and C. Reinhart. 1994. Capital Flows and Macroeconomic Management: Tequila Lessons. *International Journal of Finance and Economics* 1 (3): 207–224.

Chang, Roberto, and Andres Velasco. 2001. A Model of Financial Crises in Emerging Markets. *Quarterly Journal of Economics* 116 (2): 489–517.

Chari, V., and R. Jagannathan. 1988. Banking Panics, Information, and Rational Expectations Equilibrium. *Journal of Finance* 43 (3): 749–761.

Chen, Y. 1999. Banking Panics: The Role of the First-Come, First-Served Rule and Information Externalities. *Journal of Political Economy* 107 (5): 946–968.

Chinn, M., and K. Kletzer. 2000. International Capital Inflows, Domestic Financial Intermediation and Financial Crises Under Imperfect Information. *NBER Working Paper No. 7902*. National Bureau of Economic Research (NBER), Cambridge, September.

Diamond, Douglas W., and Philip H. Dybvig. 1983. Bank Runs, Deposit Insurance, and Liquidity. *Journal of Political Economy* 91 (3): 401–419.

Diamond, Douglas W., and Raghuram Rajan. 2002. Liquidity Shortages and Banking Crises. *NBER Working Paper No. 8937*. NBER, Cambridge, May.

Dooley, Michael P. 2000. A Model of Crises in Emerging Markets. *Economic Journal* 110: 256–272.

Fischer, Stanley. 2002. Financial Crises and the Reform of the International Financial System. *NBER Working Paper No. 9297*. NBER, Cambridge, October.

Flood, Robert P., and Peter M. Garber. 1984. Collapsing Exchange-Rate Regimes: Some Linear Examples. *Journal of International Economics* 17: 1–13.

Gorton, G. 1988. Banking Panics and Business Cycles. *Oxford Economic Papers* 40 (3): 221–255.

Honohan, Patrick, and Daniela Klingebiel. 2000. Controlling Fiscal Costs of Banking Crises. *World Bank Working Paper No. 2441*. World Bank, Washington DC, September.

Jacklin, C., and S. Bhattacharya. 1988. Distinguishing Panics and Information-Based Bank Runs: Welfare and Policy Implications, *Journal of Political Economy* 96 (June): 568–592.

Johnson, Simon, Peter Boone, Alasdair Breach, and Eric Friedman. 2000. Corporate Governance in the Asian Financial Crisis. *Journal of Financial Economics* 58 (4): 141–186.

Kindleberger, C. 1978. *Manias, Panics and Crashes: A History of Financial Crises*. New York: Basic Books.

Krueger, Anne O. 2002. *A New Approach to Sovereign Debt Restructuring*. Washington DC: International Monetary Fund.

Krugman, Paul. 1979. A Model of Balance-of-Payments Crises. *Journal of Money, Credit, and Banking* 11 (3): 311–325.

———. 1997. Are Currency Crises Self-Fulfilling? *NBER Macroeconomics Annual*. 345–378. Cambridge, MA: MIT Press.

———. 1998. What happened to Asia? *Mimeo*. Available: web.mit.edu/krugman/www/disinter.html

———. 1999. Balance Sheets, the Transfer Problem, and Financial Crises. In *International Finance and Financial Crises: Essays in Honor of Robert P. Flood Jr.*, edited by Peter Isard, Assaf Razin, and Andrew K. Rose. Norwell, MA: Kluwer Academic Publishers.

Miller, Marcus, and Lei Zhang. 2000. Sovereign Liquidity Crises: The Strategic Case for a Payments Standstill. *Economic Journal* 110 (460): 335–362.

Miron, J. 1985. Financial Panics, the Sensitivity of the Nominal Interest Rate and the Founding of the Fed. *American Economic Review* 76 (1): 125–140.

Mishkin, F. 1996. Understanding Financial Crises: A Developing Country Perspective. *NBER Working Paper No. 5600*. NBER, Cambridge, May.

Obstfeld, Maurice. 1986. Rational and Self-Fulfilling Balance of Payments Crises. *American Economic Review* 76: 72–81.

———. 1996. Models of Currency Crises with Self-Fulfilling Features. *European Economic Review* 40 (3–5): 1037–1047.

Sachs, Jeffrey. 1994a. Russia's Struggle with Stabilization: Conceptual Issues and Evidence. In *Proceedings of the Annual Conference on Development Economics*, edited by Michael Bruno and Boris Pleskovic, 57–80. Washington DC: World Bank.

———. 1994b. Beyond Bretton Woods: A New Blueprint. *The Economist* 333 (1–7 October): 23, 25, 27.

Salant, Stephen, and Dale Henderson. 1978. Market Anticipation of Government Policy and the Price of Gold. *Journal of Political Economy* 86: 627–648.

CHAPTER

3

Predicting Financial Crises: An Overview

Morris Goldstein[1]

3.1 Introduction

This paper aims to provide an overview of the progress in developing and applying early warning systems (EWS) for financial (banking and currency) crises in emerging economies. Investing in the development of an early warning model is important for two reasons. First, banking and currency crises are extremely costly to the countries in which they originate—as well as to other countries that are affected by the spillover of the original crisis.

In the case of systemic banking crises, there have been more than 100 episodes in 93 countries since the late 1970s (Caprio and Honohan 2001). In about a dozen and a half of these occurring in developing countries, the public sector resolution costs have amounted to 10% or more of the country's gross domestic product (GDP). One estimate put the total bailout costs of banking crises in developing countries at US$250 billion since 1980—and that was before the Asian crisis (Honohan 1997). In addition to the enormous fiscal costs, banking crises worsen recessions, prevent national savings from flowing to their most productive use, constrain monetary policy options, and increase the probability of a currency crisis.

An International Monetary Fund (IMF) study (1998) reported that it takes about three years for output growth to return to trend after the outbreak of a banking crisis and that the cumulative output loss averages 12%. Recent

[1] The author would like to acknowledge that this chapter draws heavily from an earlier collegial work (Goldstein, Kaminsky, and Reinhart 2000).

findings by the World Bank (2000) indicate that one in three banking crises in developing countries results in a cumulative output loss of 20% of GDP or more.

Turning to monetary policy, the main reason the Mexican authorities did not raise interest rates after the Colosio assassination in early 1994 was that banking problems had already become serious and they were worried that a rise in interest rates would push banks over the edge. Yet failure to raise interest rates in the face of declining investor confidence and a rapid fall in international reserves ultimately led to a currency and debt crisis (Calvo and Goldstein 1996). A central bank confronted with serious banking problems will not be able to make interest rate decisions in the same way as when the banking system is healthy.

The early warning literature also indicates that the presence of a banking crisis is one of the best leading indicators of a currency crisis. The cost of currency crises likewise has been shown to be significant. Mexico's peso crisis was accompanied in 1995 by a decline in real GDP of 6%—its deepest recession in 60 years. In emerging Asia, consensus forecasts for 1998 growth issued just prior to the crisis (in May/June 1997) generally stood in the 6–8% range. But the actual outcomes were unprecedented recessions (Goldstein 1998). The IMF (1998) estimated that emerging economies suffer, on average, an 8% cumulative loss in real output during a severe currency crisis.

There is also the "contagious" characteristic of crises. Although the contagion of financial disturbances usually runs from large countries to smaller ones, the Asian financial crisis demonstrated that severe financial sector difficulties in even a relatively small economy (namely Thailand) can have wide ranging spillover effects if it acts as a "wake-up call" for investors to reassess country risk, and if a set of other economies has vulnerabilities similar to those in the initial economy affected (Goldstein 1998). Currency crises can also exhibit contagion behavior. One study found that a currency crisis somewhere in the world increased the probability of a second speculative attack elsewhere by about 7%—even after controlling for economic and political fundamentals of the country concerned.

The more costly it is to clean up a financial crisis, the greater the returns to designing a well-functioning EWS.

The second reason for investing in an EWS is that a simple look at traditional market indicators of currency and default risks frequently will not provide much advance warning of an impending crisis.

Current evidence suggests that the performance of interest spreads and credit ratings was disappointing in the run-up to the Asian financial crisis. Examining interest rate spreads on 3-month offshore securities, one study found that these spreads gave no warning of impending difficulties for Indonesia, Malaysia, and Philippines, i.e., they were either flat or declining, and produced only intermittent signals for Thailand. A recent analysis of spreads using local interest rates for Korea, Malaysia, and Thailand similarly found little indication of growing crisis vulnerability.

Sovereign credit ratings on long-term, foreign-currency debt issued by the two largest international ratings firms were even less prescient in the Asian crisis. There were almost no downgrades for the most severely affected countries in the 18-month run-up to the crisis. As *The Economist* (1997) put it, "... in country after country, it has often been the case of too little, too late." Goldstein, Kaminsky, and Reinhart (2000) showed that the experience of the Asian crisis is not atypical. Neither interest rate spreads nor sovereign credit ratings ranked high in a long list of early warning indicators of currency and systemic banking crises.

If market participants expect an official bailout of a troubled borrower, then the interest rate is going to reflect the creditworthiness of the guarantor—not the troubled borrower. In such cases, interest rates are not going to be good at anticipating difficulties. Similarly, if credit ratings take into account the probability of the borrower receiving a bailout, they will also be handicapped as an early warning indicator. If market participants are not able to obtain timely and comprehensive information on the creditworthiness of banks and their clients, many otherwise-useful early warning indicators are not apt to function well in practice.

Problems also exist in anticipating problems and failures at individual banks in emerging economies. One recent study that analyzed banking problems in Colombia (1991–1998), Mexico (1993–1994), Venezuela (1993–1994), and Korea, Malaysia, and Thailand (each in 1996–1997) reported that traditional indicators of bank fragility, such as ratios of capital to assets, net profit margins, operating costs to assets, and liquidity ratios, did a relatively poor job of isolating subsequent problem banks (Rojas-Suarez 2001). The author argued that this result was no accident. If accounting standards and reporting systems are weak, classification of nonperforming loans (NPLs) is lax, an underprovision of reserves against credit losses exists, supervisory actions under the law are not enforced when performance is deemed faulty, and there is an absence of liquid and deep capital markets, then it will be difficult to validate the true value of bank capital as distinct from the accounting value, i.e., traditional CAMEL-type ratios—capital adequacy, asset quality, management soundness, earnings, and liquidity—will not anticipate difficulties at individual banks. Rojas-Suarez (2001) found instead that, in this environment, the interest rate on bank deposits is a better leading indicator.

Similarly, both Calomiris and Powell (2000) and Peria and Schmukler (1999) showed that bank deposit volumes and interest rates on deposits have provided useful information on banks' creditworthiness and the *ex post* incidence of bank failures in some emerging economies in Latin America when the official safety net is limited and investors face a real prospect of losses. But these indicators do not provide good signals when these same conditions are not present.

Karacadag and Shrivastava (2000) have argued persuasively that asset prices, including yields on subordinated bank debt, may not provide a good signal of banking problems in many developing countries if disclosure and audit systems are inadequate, if there is a lack of sizable nonbank financial intermediaries, and if there is a high risk of market manipulation associated with concentrated ownership structures and legal shortcomings. These problems still exist in East Asia as well as in several other regions.

In short, it is unlikely to get a good EWS "on the cheap" by just focusing on one or two one-size-fits-all indicators. Success is more likely if there is investment in a comprehensive EWS.

The next section provides some broad guidelines for conducting an early warning exercise. Section 3 reviews several key methodological issues. This is followed in Section 4 by a summary of some representative findings from the early warning literature. Section 5 identifies some future extensions of existing work. Finally, Section 6 addresses some criticisms of early warning models.

3.2 Broad Guidelines for an Early Warning Exercise

The following are some helpful guidelines for designing an approach to identify early warning indicators of financial crises, as drawn from Goldstein, Kaminsky, and Reinhart (2000).

First, finding a systematic pattern in the origin of financial crises means looking beyond the last prominent crisis (or group of crises) to a larger sample. Otherwise there is a risk that there will be too many potential explanations to discriminate between important and less important factors, or that generalizations will be drawn that do not necessarily apply across a wider body of experience. To guard against these risks, Goldstein, Kaminsky, and Reinhart (2000) looked at a sample of 87 currency crises and 29 banking crises in 25 emerging economies and smaller industrial countries during 1970–1995. Looking at just a single case may not provide much information.

Consider the 1994–1995 Mexican peso crisis. Was the crisis primarily driven by Mexico's large current account deficit (equal to almost 8% of GDP in 1994) and by the overvaluation of the peso's real exchange rate, or by the maturity and composition of Mexico's external borrowing (too much short-term and too dependent on portfolio flows), or by the uses to which that foreign borrowing was put (too much for consumption and not enough for investment), or by the already weakened state of the banking system (the share of NPLs doubled between mid-1990 and mid-1994), or by bad luck (in the form of unfortunate domestic political developments and the upward turn in US interest rates), or by delays in correcting earlier slippages in monetary and fiscal policies in the face of market nervousness, or by other things? Generalization about what is important and what is not cannot be made based on only one or two cases.

Looking from the opposite perspective, there is a risk of "jumping the gun" by generalizing prematurely about the relative importance of particular indicators from a relatively small set of prominent crises. An example is "credit booms," i.e., expansions of bank credit that are large relative to the growth of the economy. These have been shown to be a precursor of banking crises in Japan, several Scandinavian countries, and Latin America. However, a comparison of credit booms as a leading indicator of banking crises to other indicators across a larger group of emerging economies and smaller industrial countries indicated that credit booms were outperformed by many other indicators. Similarly, overvaluation of the real exchange rate may not have been the key factor in the Asian crisis of 1997–1998, but it still could be the best on average among a set of leading indicators in a larger sample of currency crises.

A second guideline is to pay as much attention to banking crises as to currency crises. Most existing literature on leading indicators of financial crises relates exclusively to currency crises. Yet the costs of banking crises in developing countries appear to be greater than those of currency crises. Banking crises seem to be one of the more important factors generating currency crises. The determinants and leading indicators of banking crises should be amenable to the same type of quantitative analysis as for currency crises. To explore the interactions among banking and currency crises, Goldstein, Kaminsky, and Reinhart (2000) analyzed them separately.

A third guideline is to select the frequency of the data in line with the purposes of the study. In contrast to many other researchers, Goldstein, Kaminsky, and Reinhart (2000) employed monthly data to analyze both banking and currency crises. Use of monthly (as opposed to annual) data involves a trade-off. On the minus side, because monthly data on the requisite variables are available for fewer countries than would be the case for annual data, the decision to go with higher frequency data is likely to result in a smaller sample. However, monthly data provide more information about the timing of early warning indicators, including differences among indicators in the first arrival and persistence of signals. If the purpose is just to "explain" financial crises *ex post*, annual data can be used—but that is not an early warning exercise.

A fourth guideline is to include a relatively wide array of early warning indicators. Because there are many sources of financial crises in emerging economies, numerous indicators are needed to cover the potential suspects.

A review of the crisis literature confirms that there are many crisis "stories" (see Chapter 2). Some involve asymmetric information and "bank runs" that stress liquidity/currency mismatches and shocks that induce investors to run to liquidity or quality. Others involve inherent instability and bandwagon stories that emphasize excessive credit creation and unsound finance during the expansion phase of the business cycle. Still others are best classified as premature financial liberalization stories that focus on the perils of liberalization when banking supervision is weak and when an extensive network of explicit and implicit government guarantees produces an asymmetric payoff for increased risk taking. And finally, there are first-, second-, and third-generation models (stories) of the vulnerability of fixed exchange rates to speculative attacks on currencies and interactions of various kinds between currency and banking crises.

A fifth guideline is to employ out-of-sample tests to help gauge the usefulness of leading indicators. The in-sample performance of a model may convey a misleading sense of optimism about how well it will perform outside the sample. A good case in point is the experience of the 1970s with structural models of exchange rates for the major currencies. While these models fit well in sample, subsequent research indicated that their out-of-sample performance was no better—and often worse—than that of "naïve" models, e.g., using the spot rate or the forward rate to predict the next period's exchange rate (Meese and Rogoff 1983). Goldstein, Kaminsky, and Reinhart (2000) used data from the 1970–1995 period to calculate optimal thresholds for the indicators, but they saved data from 1996 through end-1997 to assess the out-of-sample performance of the signaling approach, including the ability to identify the countries most affected during the Asian financial crisis.

3.3 Key Methodological Issues

There are several key methodological issues that require clarification in implementing the approach to financial vulnerability assessments.

The first issue is how to define currency and banking crises. Goldstein, Kaminsky, and Reinhart (2000) define a currency crisis as a situation in which an attack on the currency leads to substantial reserve losses and/or to a sharp depreciation of the currency (if the speculative attack is ultimately successful). This definition has the advantage of being comprehensive enough to capture not only speculative attacks on fixed exchange rates, e.g., Thailand's experience prior to 2 July 1997, but also attacks that force a large devaluation beyond the established rules of a crawling peg regime or an exchange rate band, e.g., Indonesia's widening of the band prior to its flotation of the rupiah on 14 August 1997. Since reserve losses also count, the index also captures unsuccessful speculative attacks, e.g., Argentina's reserve losses in the wake of the Mexican 1994 peso crisis.

Goldstein, Kaminsky, and Reinhart (2000) constructed an index of currency market turbulence as a weighted average of exchange rate changes and reserve changes. Interest rates were excluded as many emerging markets in their sample had interest rate controls through much of the sample. The index is a weighted average of the rate of change of the exchange rate ($\dot{ER}$), and of foreign reserves ($\dot{FR}$) with weights such that the two components of the index have equal sample volatilities.

Two approaches have dominated the literature on the definition of banking crises. In one approach, a banking crisis exists if one or more of three criteria are fulfilled: (i) the ratio of NPLs to total loans in the banking system exceeds 10%; (ii) the cost of the bank rescue operation was at least 2% of GDP; and (iii) the rescue episode involved either a large-scale nationalization of banks, or extensive runs on bank deposits, or other emergency measures such as deposit freezes, bank holidays, and the issuance of government blanket guarantees (see, for example, Demirgüç-Kunt and Detragiache 1998). This approach is useful for an *ex post* analysis of banking crises, i.e., an analysis fairly far removed from the time of a crisis. A second approach that is more useful for a forecasting exercise with considerable time constraints (but which is also subject to larger errors) is to call an episode a banking crisis if there are indications of large-scale bank runs, bank closures and mergers, or large public-sector takeovers of banks—without relying on a specific quantitative guideline to define "large."

The most difficult task in defining banking crises is how to figure out when a banking crisis ends. Is it over when deposits and/or bank credit growth to the private sector return to normal, or when the NPL ratio recedes to normal levels, or when investment as a share of GDP normalizes, or when real output growth returns to trend? Illustrative of the problems involved, a recent World Bank study by Demirgüç-Kunt, Detragiache, and Gupta (2001), looking at 32 banking crises in 35 countries during 1980–1995, found that

(i) demand deposits were significantly lower (vis-à-vis the precrisis period) only in the crisis year (not thereafter), (ii) the investment share in GDP was different (lower) only in the first postcrisis year, (iii) credit growth was significantly lower in both the crisis year and the three postcrisis years, and (iv) output growth was significantly lower only in the crisis year and the first postcrisis year. In other words, one would get a different end to a banking crisis depending on which of the four measuring rods mentioned above is selected.

A second key methodological issue is how to define the "early" in early warning. For currency crises, Goldstein, Kaminsky, and Reinhart (2000) defined "early" as between 1 and 24 months before the beginning of a crisis. For banking crises, they adopted a less demanding definition of "early," namely, either from 1 to 12 months before the start of a crisis or up to 12 months after the beginning of a crisis. There are two reasons for this: (i) banking crises typically last 4–5 years and (ii) the peak of banking crises often occurs several years after they start. As such, there is some benefit in getting a warning even after a crisis begins.

In much of the literature on banking crises in emerging economies, the issue of defining "early" is not essential because the purpose of the exercise is to explain banking crises *ex post*—not to forecast them. When early warning is not involved, no distinction is usually made between contemporaneous and leading indicators of crises.

A third methodological issue is how to select the "leading indicators" for the analysis. As noted earlier, Goldstein, Kaminsky, and Reinhart (2000) chose 25 indicators—using the literature on the origins of currency and banking crises as their guide. A few examples would make this point clearer.

If the influence of bank runs and of liquidity and currency mismatches on crisis vulnerability needs to be captured, variables that make depositors and creditors nervous could be considered, i.e., variables that capture a negative shock to an economy, or declining creditworthiness of bank customers, or trouble at other banks, or growing gaps between liquid liabilities and liquid assets. Such variables might include negative changes in the country's terms of trade, a decline in exports, a domestic recession, a withdrawal of deposits at other banks, a rise in the ratio of broad money (M2) to international reserves, and a high share of short-term flows in net private capital flows.

Alternatively, suppose the objective is to give concrete representation to the theme that financial crises are driven by excessive credit creation and unsound finance during the expansion phase of a business cycle, only to come crashing down when the bubble bursts. In this case, variables (indicators) like the rate of credit expansion, or excess money balances, or declines in equity and property prices could be examined.

If the purpose is to explain currency crises that stressed misalignment of exchange rates, one could consider the depreciation of the real exchange rate from the equilibrium rate (where the equilibrium rate is measured by a 10-year trend of the actual real exchange rate).

Picking up yet other themes, the set of indicators may be selected from those suggested by various models of speculative attacks on exchange rates. More specifically, drawing on so-called "first-generation" models of speculative attacks, indicators that point to an inconsistency between monetary policy and the stock of international reserves may be chosen. In second-generation models, variables that increase the cost of defending an exchange rate target, such as a rise in interest rates, or a recession, or the presence of banking fragility, may be considered. For third-generation models, the relevant variables could be those that help capture the balance-sheet effect of depreciations—like ratios of short-term external debt to foreign reserves or the ratio of M2 balances to foreign reserves.

Another way would be to take the cue on indicators from the seeming link between financial liberalization and banking crises. Then one can select as leading indicators proxies for financial liberalization, such as a rise in the money multiplier (which often occurs after countries reduce bank reserve requirements) or a rise in the real interest rate (which often occurs in emerging economies after financial liberalization).

A fourth key methodological issue is how to identify the best individual leading indicators and how to estimate crisis probabilities—both across countries and over time. There are essentially two ways to approach this issue. One approach is the regression format. The dependent variable would then take on the value of one or zero, corresponding respectively to crisis or no-crisis observations. A logit or probit model would be estimated to find out which indicators are significant, and the estimated value of the dependent variable would be used to infer crisis probability.

The other format is the so-called signaling approach, developed by Kaminsky and Reinhart (1999). This is a nonparametric model. The basic premise of the signaling approach is that the economy behaves differently on the eve of financial crises and that this aberrant behavior has a recurrent systematic pattern. A signal is a departure from normal behavior in an indicator. If an indicator sends a signal that is followed by a crisis within a plausible time frame, it is called a good signal. If the signal is not followed by a crisis within that interval of time, it is called a false signal, or "noise." Good (bad) indicators are those with low (high) noise-to-signal ratios.

The signaling approach seeks to find an "optimal threshold" for each indicator that maximizes the forecasting ability of that indicator. Under the signaling approach, the probability of a crisis is derived from a weighted average of indicators that have crossed the optimal threshold, where the weights are the past forecasting ability of the indicators. Periods of high crisis vulnerability are those where many indicators have crossed their optimal thresholds. For example, if 12 of 25 indicators are "flashing" for country A, i.e., they have reached their optimal thresholds, versus 18 flashing for country B, we would conclude that country B is more vulnerable to a crisis than country A (assuming that flashing indicators for country B are just as reliable as those for country A). Similarly, if many more indicators are flashing in country A in late 1995 than in late 1993, then we conclude that 1995 was the time of higher crisis vulnerability.

Is the signaling approach better than the regression approach, or vice versa? This is yet to be resolved. On one hand, the signaling approach may be simpler in an informal context. On the other, it imposes certain nonlinearity restrictions on the way that indicators affect crisis probabilities—an indicator elicits a warning only once it crosses the threshold. It may be that these restrictions will be rejected by the data (Berg and Pattillo 1999). It could also turn out that it makes sense to combine the signaling approach and the regression approach—by using the signaling approach to identify the best individual leading indicators and using the regression format to calculate crisis probabilities. Only time and further research will tell.

3.4 Representative Findings from the Literature

Goldstein, Kaminsky, and Reinhart (2000) provide some empirical results from their application of the early warning models to data. The following are nine representative findings drawn from their study.

First, banking and currency crises in emerging markets do not typically arrive without any warning. There are recurring behavior patterns in the period leading up to them. Reflecting this tendency, the better indicators anticipate between 50% and 90% of the banking and currency crises that occurred over a 26-year sample period. At the same time, even the best leading indicators send a significant share of false alarms (on the order of one false alarm for every two to four true signals). In other words, the main problem is not failing to see crises that subsequently occur, but seeing more crises than those that actually occur.

Second, using monthly data, banking crises in emerging economies are more difficult to forecast accurately than currency crises. Within the sample, the average noise-to-signal ratio is higher for banking crises than for currency crises, and the model likewise does considerably better out of sample in predicting currency crises than banking crises. It is not yet clear why this is so, but a few of the likely reasons are discussed in Section 3.5.

Third, there is wide variation in performance across leading indicators, with the best-performing indicators displaying noise-to-signal ratios that are in the neighborhood of two to three times better than those for the worst performing ones.

Fourth, for currency crises, the best of the monthly indicators were an appreciation of the real exchange rate (relative to trend), a banking crisis, a decline in equity prices, a fall in exports, a high ratio of M2 to international reserves, and a recession. Among annual indicators, the two best performers were both current-account indicators, namely, a large current-account deficit relative to GDP and to investment.

Turning to banking crises, the best (in descending order) of the 15 monthly indicators were an appreciation of the real exchange rate (relative to trend), a decline in equity prices, a rise in the money multiplier, a decline in real output, a fall in exports, and a rise in the real interest rate. Among the eight annual indicators tested, the best of the pack were a high ratio of short-term capital flows to GDP and a large current-account deficit relative to investment.

Taking a broader view of "macro" studies of banking crises—and not distinguishing between contemporaneous and leading indicators, Bell (2000) concluded that banking sector problems are associated with high real interest rates, low output growth, rapid domestic credit growth, weakening terms of trade, and high inflation. The overlap with the best leading indicators of banking crises is thus only partial.

Fifth, while there is a good deal in common between the best-performing leading indicators for banking and currency crises, there is enough distinction to warrant treating the two separately.

Sixth, changes in sovereign credit rating performed considerably worse than the better leading indicators of economic fundamentals in anticipating both currency and banking crises in emerging economies. It must be noted, however, that the data of Goldstein, Kaminsky, and Reinhart (2000) on sovereign credit ratings covered only a subsample of crises and only related to two private credit rating firms (Moody's Investors Service and Institutional Investor).

Seventh, in most banking and currency crises, a high proportion of the monthly leading indicators—on the order of 50–75%—reach their signaling thresholds. Indeed, both in and out of sample, less than one sixth of the crises occurred with only five or fewer of the 15 monthly leading indicators flashing. In other words, when an emerging economy is lurching toward a financial crisis, many of the wheels come off simultaneously.

Eighth, the initial results on the testing of leading indicators out of sample have been encouraging—at least for currency crises. Goldstein, Kaminsky, and Reinhart (2000) considered two out-of-sample periods: an 18-month period running from the beginning of 1996 to end-June 1997 (just prior to the outbreak of the Asian financial crisis), and a 24-month period running from January 1996 to end–December 1997. In each period, the focus was on the ordinal ranking of countries according to their crisis vulnerability. The results of the two out-of-sample periods were quite similar.

For example, from January 1996 to June 1997, the five most vulnerable countries according to the model were South Africa, Czech Republic, Thailand, Korea, and Philippines. Of these five countries, four had crises during that period and the only one that did not, South Africa, had its crisis in July 1998. Of the five countries judged to be least vulnerable to crises, namely, Argentina, Venezuela, Uruguay, Turkey, and Peru, none had currency crises during that period. Of the Asian crisis countries, the signaling approach placed three of them—Thailand, Korea, and Philippines—in the top five vulnerability group and another one, Malaysia, in the upper third of the vulnerability rankings.

One Asian crisis country where the signaling approach did quite poorly was Indonesia. It was only ranked about midway in crisis vulnerability—yet it had the most severe crisis. Why did the model miss? The explanation probably lies in two areas. First, most of the best-performing (higher-weight) leading indicators were not flashing in Indonesia's case. For example, in mid-1997 (just before the outbreak of the crisis in Thailand), the real effective exchange rate of the Indonesian rupiah was only 4% above its long-term average and far below its critical threshold. Similarly, neither the decline in equity prices, nor the decline in exports, nor the change in the ratio of M2 to international reserves, had hit their threshold values. Second, at least three of the factors important in the Indonesian crisis were not included in the list of indicators, namely, currency/liquidity mismatches on the part of the corporate sector, regional cross-country contagion effects, and political instabilities (in this case associated with the Suharto regime). The ADB model (see Chapter 4 of this volume) did much better in forecasting the Indonesian crisis.

Nevertheless, the out-of-sample performance of the model by Goldstein, Kaminsky, and Reinhart (2000) was encouraging—especially given the well-documented failure of private credit ratings and interest rate spreads to anticipate these Asian currency crises (with the possible exception of Thailand), and given that these forecasts are based solely on own-country fundamentals, i.e., with no help from contagion variables. In this sense, the model can serve as a useful first screen for detecting large ordinal differences in crisis vulnerability across countries. Some other researchers—including Furman and Stiglitz (1998), and Berg and Pattillo (1999)—found that the out-of-sample performance of the signals model was not as favorable as suggested by Goldstein, Kaminsky, and Reinhart (2000). The reason could be that these other researchers used a more stringent measuring rod to assess performance than that of the latter. It could also reflect a host of other (at this stage) unknown factors.

On the banking side, the signaling approach did not do as well. Of the five countries rated most vulnerable by the model, only two had crises during the out-of-sample period. Again, of the five countries rated least vulnerable to crises, none actually experienced a crisis.

Ninth, cross-country contagion adds importantly to country-specific fundamentals in understanding emerging-market vulnerability to currency crises. Contagion is defined as a case where the presence of a crisis elsewhere increases the probability of a crisis at home, even when the fundamentals have been taken into account. Goldstein, Kaminsky, and Reinhart (2000) considered four channels through which shocks can be transmitted across borders. Two channels dealt with trade links (bilateral trade flows and trade competition in third-country markets), and two channels addressed financial links (correlation of asset returns in global portfolios and reliance on a common bank lender). They demonstrated how these four contagion channels could be combined and weighted appropriately to form a contagion vulnerability index (CVI). According to the CVI, Argentina and Brazil had high contagion vulnerability to the 1994 Mexican peso crisis; Indonesia, Korea, and Malaysia had high vulnerability to the 1997 Thai crisis; and Argentina, Chile, and Uruguay had high vulnerability to the 1999 Brazilian crisis. Although it is difficult to separate financial contagion channels from trade channels (as countries linked in trade are also linked in finance), the conclusion was that withdrawal of a common bank lender (particularly Japanese banks) and high correlation of asset returns were important in the contagion in Asia in 1997–1998.

3.5 Extensions of and Problems with Early Warning Modeling

Early warning modeling could be extended and improved further. First, there is a need to find better models for forecasting banking crises in emerging economies. As noted earlier, the signaling approach does considerably better with currency crises than with banking crises. Part of this arises from the difficulty of dating banking crises accurately, but much of it is attributable to the absence of indicators that capture the institutional, ownership, and incentive aspects of bank fragility. In short, one cannot forecast banking crises well by just using macro variables.

There is considerable empirical work—much of which from the World Bank—that suggests banking fragility is higher when there is a large share of banking assets in state banks; when there are significant entry barriers to foreign banks; when banking systems are small; and when banks cannot engage in securities, insurance, and real estate activities (see, for example, the evidence summarized in Caprio and Honohan 2001). In addition, the design of the regulatory system and incentives for private sector monitoring of banks also matter a lot (Barth, Caprio, and Levine 2001). So far, these variables that summarize the institutional-ownership-regulatory framework have been used exclusively to explain banking crisis vulnerability—not to forecast crises. A constraint is that the actual data are only available at low frequencies—either annual or only for selected benchmark years. Forecasting banking crises can be improved if the cross-section institutional empirical literature is integrated with the high-frequency, macro, early-warning literature. For example, the institutional variables can be used to get an ordinal ranking of vulnerability across countries, and then the macro variables can be used to get a handle on the likely timing of crises, i.e., when crisis vulnerability increases sharply for a particular country. Combining the two literatures is not easy but would be well worth a try.

A second useful extension would be to increase our understanding of the channels of cross-country crisis contagion. More specifically, it may be useful to explore contagion linked to what may be called the "wake-up call" hypothesis, as well as to liquidity deficiencies across asset markets, and to common risk-management practices (Goldstein 1998).

The wake-up-call contagion refers to a situation where investors ignore certain crisis vulnerabilities until the crisis occurs. They then "wake up" and punish countries that have vulnerabilities perceived to be similar to those in the original crisis country. The question then is how to model such contagion via similar country characteristics.[2]

Liquidity of bond and equity markets can matter because industrial country fund managers faced with redemptions may sell off the most liquid emerging-market securities first—even if those countries have little other connection to the original crisis country.

[2] An impressive start in modeling wake-up-call contagion can be found in Ahluwalia (2000).

Also, if investors are subject to the same value-at-risk regulatory system and they suffer a loss from an emerging market currency or banking crisis, the common response might be a cutback in exposure, including that to other emerging economies. This reduction in exposure could increase vulnerability elsewhere.

It remains to be seen whether these more exotic contagion channels will be nearly as important as traditional contagion via bilateral trade and finance channels or via dependence on a common bank lender. Nevertheless, cross-country contagion should be viewed as a potentially multifaceted phenomenon.

A third promising extension would be to introduce some additional leading indicators into the exercise. Suggested variables are those that proxy currency mismatching, such as the ratio of short-term external debt to reserves. Currency mismatches matter not only for the probability of getting into a crisis but also for crisis severity (Goldstein 2002). Variables that might capture vulnerabilities in property lending by banks (such as the exposure of banks to the property sector and the change in real property prices) would likewise be worthy of a close look. ADB studies (see chapters 4 and 5 of this book) are already experimenting with some of these newer indicator variables.

3.6 Conclusions

Given the feasible alternatives, it would be a good investment for both the public and private sectors to put some resources into the design and testing of early warning models of financial crises. The ongoing efforts at ADB and elsewhere to build better early warning models, including those in a regional context, are steps in the right direction.

Two of the more popular criticisms of early warning models are not persuasive. One criticism is that they are completely mechanical—just brute number crunching. This is true, but their mechanical nature is also their strength. The model does not know whether or not it is a politically opportune time to blow the whistle on a particular country. It just reads the data, flashes when an indicator reaches a critical threshold, and reports the results. It does not know that the government has once again pledged to deal with its macro imbalances in the next budget cycle. The point is simply that more discretionary analysis of crisis vulnerability also has its biases and the mechanical nature of early warning models can offset some of them.

A second criticism goes in the other direction. It says that once the existence of good early warning indicators is widely known, governments will react to these signals. Hence, the models will no longer forecast crises but instead will just anticipate corrective action. If such were the case, early warning models would not work well, but there would be fewer crises and we would all be much better off.

This is not expected to happen soon. For one thing, countries may recognize crisis vulnerability but *not* take corrective action because they are adverse to both the cost of and impediments to change. Japan, for example, had high crisis vulnerability throughout much of the 1990s but did not find a way to take strong crisis prevention measures. This problem is quite widespread. For another thing, the performance of early warning models is not yet good enough for the official community to regard the forecasts of any particular early warning model as a catalyst for policy intervention. In short, we probably have a long way to go before we need to worry that the success of early warning models will lead to their demise.

References

Ahluwalia, Pavan. 2000. Discriminating Contagion: An Alternative Explanation of Contagious Currency Crises in Emerging Markets. *IMF Working Papers 00/14.* IMF, Washington DC, February.

Barth, James, Gerard Caprio, and Ross Levine. 2001. *Bank Regulation and Supervision: What Works and What Doesn't?* World Bank, Washington DC, December.

Bell, James. 2000. Leading Indicator Models of Banking Crises: A Critical Review. *Bank of England Financial Stability Review* (9): 113–129.

Berg, Andrew, and Catherine Pattillo. 1999. Are Currency Crises Predictable: A Test. *IMF Staff Papers* 46 (2).

Calomiris, Charles, and Andrew Powell. 2000. Can Emerging Market Bank Regulators Establish Credible Discipline: The Case of Argentina. *NBER Working Paper No. 7715.* National Bureau of Economic Research (NBER), Cambridge, May.

Calvo, Guillermo, and Morris Goldstein. 1996. What Role for the Official Sector? In *Private Capital Flows to Emerging Markets After the Mexican Crisis,* edited by Guillermo Calvo, Eduard Hochreiter, and Morris Goldstein. Washington DC: Institute for International Economics.

Caprio, Gerard, and Patrick Honohan. 2001. *Finance and Growth: Policy Choices in a Volatile World.* Washington DC: World Bank.

Demirgüç-Kunt, A., and E. Detragiache. 1998. The Determinants of Banking Crises in Developing and Developed Countries. *IMF Staff Papers* 45 (1).

Demirgüç-Kunt, A., E. Detragiache, and P. Gupta. 2001. Inside the Crisis: An Empirical Analysis of Banking Systems in Distress. *World Bank Policy Research Paper No. 2431*. World Bank, Washington DC.

The Economist. 1997. Why Risk is No Longer a Four Letter Word. 28 August.

Furman, Jason, and Joseph Stiglitz. 1998. Economic Crises: Evidence and Insights from East Asia. *Brookings Papers on Economic Activity* 1998: 2 (June).

Goldstein, Morris. 1998. *The Asian Financial Crisis: Causes, Consequences, and Systemic Implications*. Washington DC: Institute for International Economics.

———. 2002. *Managed Floating Plus and the Great Currency Regime Debate*. Washington DC: Institute for International Economics.

Goldstein, Morris, Graciela Kaminsky, and Carmen Reinhart. 2000. *Assessing Financial Vulnerability: An Early Warning System for Emerging Markets*. Washington DC: Institute for International Economics.

Goldstein, Morris, and Philip Turner. 1996. Banking Crises in Emerging Economies: Origins and Policy Options. *BIS Economic Papers 46*. Bank for International Settlements (BIS), October.

Honohan, Patrick. 1997. Banking System Failures in Developing and Transition Economies. *BIS Working Papers No. 39,* BIS, Basle, January.

International Monetary Fund. 1998. *World Economic Outlook.* Washington DC: IMF.

Kaminsky, Graciela, and Carmen Reinhart.1999. The Twin Crises: The Causes of Banking and Balance-of-Payments Problems. *American Economic Review* 89 (3): 473-500.

Karacadag, Cem, and Animesh Shrivastava. 2000. The Role of Subordinated Debt In Market Discipline: The Case of Emerging Markets. *IMF Working Paper No. 00/215*. IMF, Washington DC, December.

La Porta, R., F. Lopez-de-Salanes, and A. Shleifer. 2000. *Government Ownership of Banks*. Harvard University, Cambridge, August.

Lindgren, C., G. Garcia, and M. Saal. 1996. *Bank Soundness and Macroeconomic Policy*. Washington DC: IMF.

Meese, Richard, and Ken Rogoff. 1983. Empirical Exchange Rate Models of the Seventies: Do They Fit Out of Sample? *Journal of International Economics* 14 (February): 3–24.

Peria, M., and S. Schmukler. 1999. Do Depositors Punish Banks for "Bad" Behavior: Examining Market Discipline in Argentina, Chile, and Mexico. *World Bank Policy Research Working Paper No. 2058*. World Bank, Washington DC, February.

Rojas-Suarez, Liliana. 2001. Can International Capital Standards Strengthen Banks in Emerging Economies? *Institute for International Economics Working Paper No. 01/10.* Institute for International Economics, Washington DC, October.

World Bank. 2000. *Global Economic Prospects and the Developing Countries, 2000.* Washington DC: World Bank.

CHAPTER 4

Nonparametric EWS Models of Currency and Banking Crises for East Asia

Juzhong Zhuang

4.1 Introduction

This chapter presents two early warning system (EWS) models, one for currency crises, the other for banking crises. The two models follow the signaling approach pioneered by Kaminsky and Reinhart (1999). They are estimated using monthly data of six East Asian countries—Indonesia, Republic of Korea (Korea), Malaysia, Philippines, Singapore, and Thailand—and, therefore, may be considered "regional models." In contrast, empirical EWS models reported in existing studies were often estimated using data of 20–30 countries, including both developed and developing countries, and thus can be considered "global models."

In this chapter, we show that the two EWS models have reasonably good predictive power both in sample and out of sample. Leading indicators and composite indexes of the two models are in general more reliable and predict a higher proportion of crisis episodes than those reported elsewhere. In particular, the two models are capable of predicting episodes of the 1997 Asian financial crisis in four of the five crisis-affected countries—Indonesia, Korea, Malaysia, Philippines, and Thailand—with the currency crisis EWS outperforming the banking crisis EWS.

Three methodological extensions are made in developing the two models. First, a number of new leading indicators not used elsewhere are found to be good predictors of financial crises in the context of the six East Asian countries. Second, six sector-specific composite indexes are constructed and found useful in predicting crises and in identifying sources of financial vulnerabilities. And third, a stochastic trend is used as a proxy for the long run equilibrium level of the real exchange rate, one of the best leading indicators identified by many studies on EWS models. A stochastic trend is theoretically more acceptable and empirically easier to use, especially in *ex ante* forecasting, compared with the commonly used deterministic trend.

The rest of the chapter is organized as follows. Section 4.2 describes methodology. Section 4.3 presents the currency crisis EWS model and Section 4.4 the banking crisis EWS model. Section 4.5 looks at results of out-of-sample evaluations and asks whether the two models could have predicted the 1997 East Asian financial crisis. Finally, Section 4.6 summarizes key findings and discusses areas for further work.

4.2 Methodology

The signaling approach to developing an EWS model involves five steps: dating historical crisis episodes, selecting leading indicators as predictors of crises, setting threshold values for the selected leading indicators, constructing composite indexes, and predicting crises. This section explains technical details involved in these steps, highlights some problems of the existing method, and describes modifications made in this study to address the problems identified. Goldstein, Kaminsky, and Reinhart (2000) provide more details.

Dating Historical Crisis Episodes

The first step in developing an EWS system is to determine what constitutes a crisis and, based on this definition, to date historical crisis episodes. Both currency and banking crises are considered.

CURRENCY CRISES

In the EWS literature, currency crises are often defined as episodes of significant currency depreciations (mostly against the US dollar), foreign reserve losses, and/or short-term interest rate hikes. Considering reserve losses and interest rate hikes is intended to capture unsuccessful attacks in foreign exchange markets. In practice, two methods have been used in dating episodes of currency crises. One involves constructing an exchange market pressure index. Originally proposed by Eichengreen, Rose, and Wyplosz (1994), the exchange market pressure index, in the case of monthly data, is a weighted average of month-on-month percentage changes in a bilateral nominal exchange rate, foreign reserves, and a short-term interest rate. A crisis episode is considered occurring in a particular month if this index exceeds its sample mean by a certain standard deviation, such as two or three. The other method also looks at month-on-month changes in exchange rates, foreign reserves, and interest rates in defining crises, but does so separately, and uses fixed and arbitrarily set cutoff or "trigger" points—say, 10% for currency depreciation, 20% for reserve losses, and 3 percentage points for interest rate hikes. There are pros and cons for both methods (see Box 1).

In this study, we follow the first approach, but focus only on currency depreciation. We ignore unsuccessful attacks, as the way they are modeled by the exchange market pressure index is not satisfactory. One of the problems is that there can be instances when a significant depreciation is accompanied by a large increase in foreign reserves during the same period. In such circumstances, the two would offset each other in the computation of the exchange market pressure index, possibly leading to a crisis episode being missed. Unsuccessful attacks are important and worth considering. But for policy analysis, a better way of modeling them needs to be found.[1]

In this study, therefore, a crisis episode is considered occurring in a country in a particular month if the month-on-month percentage change in the country's nominal exchange rate against the US dollar exceeds its sample mean by two standard deviations, that is,

$$\dot{ER}_t > \mu_{ER} + 2\delta_{ER} \qquad (4.1)$$

where $\dot{ER}_t$ is the month-on-month percentage change in a country's exchange rate in units of domestic currency per US dollar, μ_{ER} is the sample mean of month-on-month percentage changes in the exchange rate, and δ_{ER} is its standard deviation.

BANKING CRISES

Banking crises are more difficult to define; hence rules for dating crisis episodes are more varied (see Box 1). Nevertheless, these rules can be classified into two broad groups: indicators-based and events-based. The indicators-based rules include the use of numerical indicators such as nonperforming loan (NPL) ratios, costs of bank rescue operations, and losses of bank capital. The events-based rules involve identifying major events related to individual banks or the entire banking system, including bank runs; closures, mergers, or takeovers of major financial institutions; or public sector interventions in

[1] An examination of the data used in this study reveals that, for many countries during the sample period, a large decline in reserves in a particular month was often followed by an equally large increase in reserves the following month or months, making it difficult to judge whether the decline represented an unsuccessful attack or merely seasonal reserve fluctuations.

Box 1 **Dating Financial Crises**

The first step in developing an EWS model is to define what constitutes a crisis and then to date crisis episodes from sample data to be used as the left-hand side variable.

Currency Crises

Two methods have been used in dating crises in empirical studies. The more commonly used method involves constructing a so-called exchange market pressure index, originally proposed by Eichengreen, Rose, and Wyplosz (1994). In their work, a currency crisis is defined as large movements in exchange rates, foreign reserves, and interest rates. More recent studies on EWS models, however, have focused only on large movements in exchange rates and reserves, as historical data for short-term interest rates are often lacking, especially for emerging markets. The exchange market pressure index, in the case of monthly data, is thus often defined as a weighted average of month-on-month percentage changes in a bilateral nominal exchange rate (e.g., local currency/US dollar) and foreign reserves, with weights such that the two components of the index have equal sample volatility, that is,

$$EMP_t = \dot{ER}_t - \frac{\delta_1}{\delta_2} \dot{FR}_t$$

where EMP_t is the exchange market pressure index at time period t, δ_1 is the standard deviation of month-on-month percentage changes of a nominal exchange rate, $\dot{ER}$, and δ_2 is the standard deviation of month-on-month percentage changes of foreign reserves, $\dot{FR}$. Large movements in foreign reserves (and short-term interest rates) are included in constructing EMP_t to capture unsuccessful speculative attacks on a local currency. These could occur when government measures to defend a currency avoid sharp depreciations, but at the cost of losing a large amount of reserves. A particular month is defined as a crisis month if its EMP_t exceeds the sample mean plus, say, three standard deviations, that is,

$$EMP_t > \mu_{EMP} + 3\delta_{EMP}$$

where μ_{EMP} is the sample mean and δ_{EMP} is the standard deviation of EMP_t.

The other method uses fixed and arbitrarily set cutoff or "trigger" points that are not dependent on sample data. For instance, the Emerging Market Risk Indicator of Credit Suisse First Boston (Roy 2001) defines a currency crisis as a devaluation that is greater than 5% and at least double that of the preceding month. The Deutsche Bank Alarm Clock (Garber, Lumsdaine, and Longato 2001) uses various trigger points such as a depreciation of greater than 10% and an interest rate increase of greater than 25% in dating crises.

The first method, which takes into account the level of values of the crisis index relative to its history in a particular country, has an advantage over defining a crisis by the same absolute cutoff points for all countries. For example, for a country that has had a pegged exchange rate regime and the rate has remained fixed for some time, a relatively small devaluation may be considered a crisis. The same size depreciation might not constitute a crisis in a country where the exchange rate is flexible and has been more volatile (Berg and Pattillo 1999).

However, the first method also has its drawbacks. First, the way EMP_t is constructed makes it difficult to interpret, as the sum of weights in the formula is not equal to one. Second, there may be cases where currency devaluation is accompanied by positive growth in reserves during the same period. In such cases, crisis episodes may be missed because the positive growth of reserves could offset the exchange rate depreciation. Third, thresholds defined using the above formula are sample dependent. These drawbacks are in fact advantages of the second approach.

Banking Crises

Similar to currency crises, there are two methods used for dating banking crises in empirical studies. The more widely used is the events-based approach, which employs a combination of events to identify and date the occurrence of a banking crisis. These events usually include forced closures, mergers, or government intervention in the operations of financial institutions; bank runs; or the extension of large-scale government assistance to the banking sector. Another method uses numerical indicators such as nonperforming loans (NPLs) and cost of bank rescues as identifying criteria. In the literature, there is no consensus on the benchmark level of such indicators. For example, Sheng (1996) uses a 15% NPL threshold for identifying banking crises. On the other hand, Demirgüç-Kunt and Detragiache (1997) defined banking crises based on the criteria of NPLs exceeding 10%, or the cost of bank rescue of at least 2% of GDP.

Both methods have their advantages and limitations. A clear advantage of the events-based approach is data availability—information on dates of government intervention and changes in banking regulations is relatively easy to find. However, as pointed out by Kibritcioglu (1998), the events-based approach also has limitations: (i) identifying dates of crises is possible for annual data, but difficult for monthly data; (ii) dates of government intervention, which are often used to pinpoint crisis dates, may not necessarily reflect reality; and (iii) it is not always easy to judge whether a crisis is systemic or not, particularly if one uses information only on government intervention.

The indicators-based method has some advantages. It provides a tool for monitoring and interpreting developments in the banking sector. Based on the levels of the numerical indicators, one can define criteria to differentiate between systemic and nonsystemic crises. Its drawbacks mainly relate to data problems. Reliable monthly banking sector data may not be readily available. Available data may be biased due to reporting problems or country-specific regulations.

the banking sector. Both approaches have drawbacks. As Goldstein, Kaminsky, and Reinhart (2000) have noted, most indicators that could be used under the indicators-based rules are usually available only at low frequencies, if at all. Some indicators, such as NPL ratios, could also be made less informative by banks' desire to hide their problems for as long as possible. In the case of events-based rules, a crisis could be dated too late because financial problems usually begin well before a bank is finally closed or merged. It could also be dated too early because the worst of the crisis may come later (Goldstein, Kaminsky, and Reinhart 2000). These problems are particularly relevant for high frequency EWS models using monthly data, such as those being developed in this study.

This study uses systemic banking crisis episodes that were identified by Goldstein, Kaminsky, and Reinhart (2000) for Indonesia, Korea, Malaysia, Philippines, and Thailand. In that study, the beginning of a banking crisis was marked by two types of events: bank runs that led to closures, mergers, or public sector takeovers of one or more major financial institutions; and if there were no bank runs, then closures, mergers, takeovers of, or large-scale government assistance to an important financial institution or group of institutions that ignite a series of similar outcomes at other financial institutions.

Selecting Leading Indicators

Leading indicators as predictors of financial crises are often chosen based on economic rationale and data availability. Kaminsky, Lizondo, and Reinhart (1998) carried out a comprehensive survey of various types of leading indicators used in 15 empirical studies of currency crises. These are mostly indicators of macroeconomic fundamentals and external positions, and can be classified into capital account, debt profile, current account, international, financial liberalization, other financial, real sector, fiscal, institutional/ structural, and political categories. While they found that international reserves, real exchange rate, credit growth, credit to the public sector, and domestic inflation receive ample support as useful indicators of currency crises, with trade balance, export performance, money growth, the broad money (M2)/foreign reserves ratio, real gross domestic product (GDP) growth, and fiscal deficit receiving some support, they also noted significant variations in the predictive performance of even the same indicator across various studies.

Although causes of banking crises often differ from those of currency crises, in empirical studies, indicators used to explain or predict banking crises are not very different from those used for explaining or predicting currency crises.[2] In both cases, they are mostly macroeconomic and external position indicators. Direct measures of financial sector soundness, such as those recently developed by the International Monetary Fund (IMF)—see Box 2—are not commonly used for predicting financial crises for several reasons. The first is data constraints. Macroeconomic and external position indicators are more easily available and usually have higher frequencies and longer time series, while direct measures of financial soundness have become publicly available only recently. The limited number of observations on these direct measures makes them not very useful for explaining historical crisis episodes or predicting future crisis events. The second reason is that many indicators of financial soundness such as NPL ratios and capital adequacy are coincident or lagging indicators, rather than leading indicators. The third justification for the use of a common set of indicators for studying both currency and banking crises is that many studies show that banking crises are one of the causes of currency crises, and that currency crises can also cause banks' balance sheets to deteriorate, leading to systemic banking crises. Indeed, some crises involve both currency and banking crises, which Kaminsky and Reinhart (1999) have labeled as "twin crises."

In this paper, we follow the lead of most empirical studies, in particular Goldstein, Kaminsky, and Reinhart (2000), by applying a common set of indicators to the modeling of currency and banking crises. Table 4.1 provides a list of leading indicators used in constructing the EWS models in this chapter and their economic rationales. Most indicators are observed at monthly intervals. But some are available only on a quarterly or annual basis. For these indicators, monthly observations are interpolated from annual/quarterly data.

Some leading indicators are trended or subject to seasonality. To ensure that leading indicators are stationary and free from seasonal effects, they need to be transformed. Most EWS studies transform leading indicators by calculating changes or percentage changes in the level of each variable with respect to its level a year earlier. A potential problem with this transformation is that an indicator could stop signaling in the lead up to a crisis if it stays within the critical region for more than 12 months.[3] This is hardly desirable. Due to this problem, this study adopts a more flexible approach to indicator specification. For each leading indicator screened, with the exception of the

[2] For instance, the indicator list provided by Kaminsky, Lizondo, and Reinhart (1998) for currency crises is similar to those used by Goldstein, Kaminsky, and Reinhart (2000); Demirgüç-Kunt and Detragiache (1997); and Eichengreen and Arteta (2000) for banking crises.

[3] For example, if the ratio of short-term external debt to foreign reserves crosses its threshold and stays unchanged for 16 months, and a crisis occurs in the 17th month, there will be no signals from this indicator in the last six months prior to the crisis.

Box 2 **IMF Financial Soundness Indicators**

In response to financial crises in several economies in the 1990s, the International Monetary Fund (IMF) launched several initiatives to improve its ability to analyze a country's vulnerability to crises. In cooperation with other international organizations, national authorities, and the private sector, the IMF has been developing financial sector soundness measures—financial soundness indicators (FSIs)—and methods of analyzing them, referred to as macroprudential analysis.

FSIs are compiled to monitor the health and soundness of financial institutions and markets, and of their corporate and household counterparts. They include aggregated information on financial institutions and indicators that are representative of markets in which financial institutions operate.

Macroprudential analysis assesses and monitors the strengths and vulnerabilities of financial systems. This encompasses quantitative information from FSIs and indicators that provide a broader picture of economic and financial circumstances, such as inflation and GDP growth, along with information on the structure of a financial system, qualitative information on the institutional and regulatory framework—particularly through assessments of compliance with international financial sector standards and codes—and the outcome of stress tests. By focusing on vulnerabilities in domestic financial systems, using FSIs as the most significant statistical building block, macroprudential analysis complements EWS models, which largely focus on external vulnerabilities, using macroeconomic indicators as key explanatory variables.

The IMF proposed two sets of financial soundness indicators—a core set and an encouraged set—for periodic monitoring, and to aid compilation and dissemination efforts of national authorities. Six criteria were applied to identify the core set, with some also applied in selecting the encouraged set: the focus on core markets and institutions; analytical significance; revealed usefulness; relevance in most circumstances, i.e., not country-specific; availability; and parsimony, i.e., achieving the maximum information content with a limited number of FSIs.

The core set includes indicators for the banking sector that should have priority in future FSI compilation and monitoring. This set focuses on the banking sector and covers the main categories of bank risk following the CAMELS framework of bank supervision: capital adequacy, asset quality, management soundness, earnings, liquidity, and sensitivity to market risk (see Table B1).

The encouraged set includes additional banking indicators, as well as data on other institutions and markets that are relevant in assessing financial stability—the corporate sector, real estate markets, and nonbank financial institutions and markets. In particular, indicators of corporate health and developments in real estate markets are considered a priority in light of their analytical significance for assessing financial vulnerabilities in a wide variety of circumstances. Thus, the IMF encourages their compilation. At present, however, they are limited, but could be included in the core set in due course.

Indicators in the core set can be combined with those in the encouraged set that might be of particular relevance to the country concerned, depending on its level of financial development, institutional structure, and regional circumstances. Working

Continued on page 48

Table B1 **Financial Soundness Indicators**

Core Set	
Capital adequacy	Regulatory capital to risk-weighted assets
	Regulatory tier I capital to risk-weighted assets
Asset quality	NPLs to total gross loans
	NPLs net of provisions to capital
	Sectoral distribution of loans to total loans
	Large exposures to capital
Earnings and profitability	Return on assets
	Return on equity
	Interest margin to gross income
	Noninterest expenses to gross income
Liquidity	Liquid assets to total assets (liquid asset ratio)
	Liquid assets to short-term liabilities
Sensitivity to market risk	Duration of assets
	Duration of liabilities
	Net open position in foreign exchange to capital
Encouraged Set	
Deposit-taking institutions	Capital to assets
	Geographical distribution of loans to total loans
	Gross asset position in financial derivatives to capital
	Gross liability position in financial derivatives to capital
	Trading income to total income
	Personnel expenses to noninterest expenses
	Spread between reference lending and deposit rates
	Spread between highest and lowest interbank rate
	Customer deposits to total (noninterbank) loans
	Foreign-currency-denominated loans to total loans
	Foreign-currency-denominated liabilities to total liabilities
	Net open position in equities to capital
Market liquidity	Average bid-ask spread in the securities market[a]
	Average daily turnover ratio in the securities market[a]
Nonbank financial institutions	Assets to total financial system assets
	Assets to GDP
Corporate sector	Total debt to equity
	Return on equity
	Earnings to interest and principal expenses
	Corporate net foreign exchange exposure to equity
	Number of applications for protection from creditors
Households	Household debt to GDP
	Household debt service and principal payments to income
Real estate markets	Real estate prices
	Residential real estate loans to total loans
	Commercial real estate loans to total loans

[a] Or in other markets that are most relevant to bank liquidity, such as foreign exchange markets

(Cont'd)

with two sets of FSIs—a core set and an encouraged set—thus avoids a one-size-fits-all approach and provides a degree of flexibility when selecting indicators most relevant in assessing vulnerabilities to country-specific circumstances.

While the IMF work on measuring and analyzing FSIs has advanced substantially in recent years, more remains to be done. Further attention is expected to focus on improving indicators of the health of nonbank financial institutions and markets, analytical tools that use FSIs, international comparability of FSIs, and convergence toward best practice.

Source: *IMF Occasional Paper* No. 212, V. Sundararajan, Charles Enoch, Armida San Jose, Paul Hilberse, Russell Krueger, Marina Morretti, and Graham Slack, 8 April 2002.

Table 4.1 **Leading Indicators of Financial Crises and Economic Rationales**

Leading Indicator	Rationale
Current Account	
Current account balance/GDI Exports Imports Real effective exchange rate Real exchange rate against the US dollar Trade account balance/GDP	Weak exports, excessive import growth, and currency overvaluation could lead to deterioration in the current account, and historically have been associated with currency crises in many countries. External weaknesses and currency overvaluation could also add to the vulnerability of the banking sector as a loss of competitiveness in the external market might lead to a recession, business failures, and a decline in the quality of loans. Banking crises could lead to currency crises.
Capital Account	
Deposits in BIS banks/foreign reserves Domestic real interest rate differential from the US rate Foreign liabilities/foreign assets of the banking sector Foreign reserves M2/foreign reserves Short-term capital flows/GDP Short-term external debt/foreign reserves	With increasing globalization and financial integration, capital account problems could make a country highly vulnerable to shocks. Manifestations of capital account problems could include declining foreign reserves, excessive short-term foreign debt, maturity and currency mismatches, and capital flight.
Financial Sector	
Deposits/M2 Domestic credit/GDP Lending-deposit rate spread Loans/deposits M1/GDP	Currency and banking crises have been linked to rapid growth in credit fueled by excessive monetary expansion in many countries, while contractions in bank deposits, high domestic real interest

M2 multiplier Real commercial bank deposits Domestic real interest rate	rates, and large lending-deposit rate spreads often reflect distress and problems in the banking sector.
Real Sector	
CPI Industrial production index Stock price index	Recessions and a bursting asset price bubble often precede banking and currency crises.
Fiscal Sector	
Central bank credit to public sector/GDP Fiscal balance/GDP Government consumption/GDP Net credit to public sector/GDP	Large fiscal deficits could lead to a worsening in the current account position, which could in turn put pressure on the exchange rate.
Global Economy	
World oil price Real US dollar/yen exchange rate US real interest rate US growth rate	Foreign recessions could spill over to domestic economies and lead to domestic recessions. High world oil prices pose a danger to the current account position, and also could lead to domestic recessions. High world interest rates often induce capital outflows. For many East Asian countries, the depreciation of the Japanese yen against the US dollar could pressure domestic currencies.

BIS = Bank for International Settlements
CPI = consumer price index
GDI = gross domestic investment
GDP = gross domestic product
M1 = narrow money
M2 = broad money

real exchange rate, two forms of specifications are considered—indicator level and 12-month change (or percentage change) in the level—with selection based on predictive power. Both are selected if both have predictive power.

For the real exchange rate, most EWS studies attempt to measure deviations from its long run equilibrium level. Because it is empirically very difficult to determine what should be a country's equilibrium real exchange rate, a common practice is to use a linear, log-linear, or exponential time trend as a proxy, assuming that the equilibrium real exchange rate will change only slowly over time. A practical problem with this approach is that the estimated trend can be sensitive to which method is used. The criterion for selecting the best fit, such as R^2, may yield results that are not clear-cut. This could be a serious problem for *ex ante* forecasting as different methods may yield conflicting outcomes. Further, a linear, log-linear, or exponential trend is deterministic, which is theoretically difficult to justify.

To address these concerns, this study uses a stochastic trend as a proxy for the equilibrium real exchange rate (and real effective exchange rate), estimated from the Hodrick-Prescott (HP) filter (Enders 1995). A stochastic trend is allowed to change over time with changes in a country's economic fundamentals and, therefore, is theoretically more acceptable. It also avoids having to choose a particular functional form as required when using a deterministic trend, and hence is empirically easier to use, especially in *ex ante* forecasting. A major weakness of a stochastic trend compared with a deterministic trend is that it may mimic the behavior of actual data too closely, making the real exchange rate less likely to exhibit large deviations from its trend. One solution is to use a larger smoothing parameter than the default level set in standard statistical packages when using the HP filter.

Since the deviation of the real exchange rate from its trend has been identified as the best leading indicator of currency crises in EWS literature, we also estimate two alternative currency crisis models to see how sensitive their performance is to the use of the real exchange rate variable and its specification: the first assumes a commonly used deterministic trend for the real exchange rate, while the second excludes the real exchange rate as a leading indicator. The results of these two alternative models are reported in Appendix 4.1.

Setting Thresholds for Leading Indicators

For each leading indicator, a threshold divides its distribution into a normal region and a critical region associated with a heightened probability of crises. For each period (a month in this study), if the observed outcome of an indicator crosses the threshold and falls into the critical region, the indicator would issue a warning signal. A warning signal could be true if a crisis follows within a chosen time frame (denoted as *A*) or false if no crisis follows within the time frame (denoted as *B*). The latter is usually referred to as a Type-II error. Similarly, when the observed outcome of an indicator stays in the normal region and, hence, issues no warning signal, this could be false if a crisis follows within a chosen time frame (denoted as *C*) or true if no crisis follows within the time frame (denoted as *D*). The former is referred to as a Type-I error. The time frame chosen for determining whether a crisis signal is true or false is called a crisis window.[4] Following the common practice in EWS literature, we set the crisis window at 24 months. With a 24-month

[4] An EWS model should issue warning signals well in advance of the onset of a crisis. This lead time could vary by indicator, among crisis episodes, and across countries. But in order to classify warning signals as true or false, a maximum lead time, termed a crisis window, has to be set.

crisis window, all the sample periods can be classified into either tranquil periods, defined as those falling outside 24 months preceding each crisis episode, or precrisis periods, defined as those falling within 24 months preceding each crisis episode. As part of sensitivity analysis, we also experiment with two alternative crisis windows: 18 months and 12 months.

The trade-off between Type-I and Type-II errors can be illustrated in Table 4.2. Widening the critical region will increase the number of false signals (*B*) and hence Type-II errors, but reduce the number of missed crises (*C*) and hence Type-I errors. On the other hand, narrowing the critical region will increase the number of missed crises and hence Type-I errors, but reduce the number of false signals and hence Type-II errors. Kaminsky, Lizondo, and Reinhart (1998) proposed setting the threshold and associated critical region to minimize the so-called noise-to-signal ratio (*NSR*), which is defined as the ratio of the probability of an indicator signaling during tranquil periods to the probability of the indicator signaling during precrisis periods, that is,

$$NSR = [B/(B+D)] / [A/(A+C)] \tag{4.2}$$

where *A*, *B*, *C*, and *D* are defined as in Table 4.2.

Table 4.2 **True and False Warning Signals**

	A Crisis Follows within 24 Months	No Crisis Follows within 24 Months
Signaling	*A*	*B*
Not signaling	*C*	*D*

Empirically, the minimum *NSR* and associated threshold and critical region of each indicator are estimated using a grid search procedure. This involves calculating *NSRs* assuming different thresholds, and choosing the one corresponding to the minimum *NSR*. For some indicators, the critical region is located at the right tail of their cumulative frequency distributions, if excessive increases in their values increase the probability of crisis occurrences. For other indicators, the critical region is located at the left tail, as excessive declines in their values increase crisis probability. If the critical region is located at the left tail of a cumulative frequency distribution, the grid search is usually limited to a range of the 10–20th percentiles, while if the critical region is located at the right tail, the grid search is limited to a range of the 80–90th percentiles.[5] With a left tail critical region, an indicator issues a

[5] This is due to two considerations. First, financial crises are rare events and, hence, thresholds should be located at tails. Second, to ensure a reasonable sample size, the critical region cannot be too small.

warning signal when its value falls below the threshold. With a right tail critical region, an indicator issues a warning signal when its value exceeds the threshold. This study follows these conventions.

The threshold of each indicator identified through the grid search is uniform for countries under consideration in terms of a *percentile* of an indicator's cumulative frequency distribution. However, to control for country-specific effects that may not be related to financial vulnerabilities but nevertheless influence the indicator's absolute values, it is assumed that its frequency distribution is country-specific. Therefore, in terms of its *actual value*, each indicator has a country-specific threshold.

Signals, Noises, and Crisis Probabilities

With a threshold value, a leading indicator can be converted to a binary variable S_{it}: 1 if the actual value crosses the threshold (warning signal), or 0 if the actual value of the indicator does not cross its threshold (no warning signal). Based on historical crisis episodes, these can then be classified either true or false as shown in Table 4.2. The minimum *NSR*, calculated by pooling the sample countries together, provides a measure of the predictive power of each leading indicator. The lower this ratio, the more powerful the leading indicator is in predicting crises. If an indicator has a minimum *NSR* greater than unity, it means that the likelihood for the indicator to issue warning signals during tranquil periods is greater than for it to issue warning signals during precrisis periods. Such indicators do not have any predictive power and should be excluded.

A second, but closely related, measure of predictive power is the conditional crisis probability, which is defined as

$$CP = A/(A+B) \tag{4.3}$$

where *CP* is the probability of a crisis occurring within 24 months conditional on a warning signal being issued by a leading indicator—the higher the conditional probability, the greater the predictive power. *CP* is related to both Type-I errors (failing to issue signals with a crisis approaching) and Type-II errors (false alarms). A reduction in Type-II errors leads to a lower *B* and therefore increases *CP*, while a reduction in Type-I errors leads to a lower C and a higher *A* (given that *A*+*C* is fixed for a given sample), and hence also increases *CP*. For a leading indicator to be of any use, its conditional crisis probability should be greater than the unconditional crisis probability *UP*, that is,

$$CP > UP \tag{4.4}$$

where *UP* is fixed for a given sample and calculated as

$$UP = (A+C)/(A+B+C+D) \tag{4.5}$$

A further measure of predictive power is the share of precrisis periods (months falling in crisis windows) correctly called by a leading indicator, defined as

$$SP = A/(A+C) \tag{4.6}$$

SP is inversely related to Type-I errors. A reduction in *C* leads to an increase in *A* and, given that *A+C* is constant for a given sample, an increase in *SP*.

Lastly, if one is more concerned with whether or not a leading indicator issues warning signals prior to a crisis episode but not so much with the number of warning signals, then one can simply count the number of crises for which the leading indicator flashes at least once within their respective crisis windows. This can also be expressed as a percentage of total crisis episodes in the sample.

Constructing Composite Indexes

When the number of leading indicators selected is large, it is useful and convenient to have an aggregated measure of financial vulnerability, a so-called composite index. By aggregating individual leading indicators, a composite index contains more information and its warning signals could be more reliable than those of a single indicator.

Based on the assumption that the greater the number of leading indicators signaling a crisis, the higher the probability that such a crisis would actually occur, Kaminsky (1999) proposed several composite indexes. One such composite index, I_t, is a simple sum of binary values (0 or 1), S_{it}, of all the selected leading indicators, defined as

$$I_t = \sum_{i=1}^{n} S_{it} \tag{4.7}$$

where *n* is the number of leading indicators selected.

An alternative is to take into account differences in the predictive power of leading indicators by giving higher weights to better performing indicators (those with smaller *NSR*s), that is,

$$I_t = \sum_{i=1}^{n} \frac{S_{it}}{NSR_i} \tag{4.8}$$

Composite indexes sometimes have been criticized due to the lack of a theoretical basis, as they involve aggregating many unrelated measures of financial vulnerability using a certain weighting scheme.[6] Further, historically, causes of financial crises have varied from country to country and, within the same country, from one episode to another. It may not be realistic to expect a single composite index to capture all signs of financial vulnerabilities and crises with different causes. One way to address these concerns is to design composite indexes by source of financial vulnerability. A practical approach to doing this is to construct sector-specific composite indexes, each designed to capture a particular type of financial vulnerability or financial crisis.

In this study, therefore, we propose two general composite indexes and six sector-specific composite indexes. The two general composite indexes are

- Composite I: A weighted average of binary values of the selected leading indicators, with weights being inverses of *NSRs* of respective indicators, and
- Composite II: A simple sum of binary values of all selected leading indicators.

Although, as we will show later, Composite II has less predictive power than Composite I, it has the advantage of being less sensitive to any particular indicator malfunctioning.

The six sector composite indexes are the current account, capital account, financial sector, real sector, fiscal sector, and global economy. Each is a weighted average of the binary values of leading indicators selected for a particular sector, with weights being inverses of *NSRs* of respective indicators for the sector.

To make a composite index comparable across periods and among countries, and free from distortions due to differences in the number of available leading indicators, we divide each index obtained from using either Equation 4.7 or 4.8 by its maximum possible value in each period and express the result in percentage. A composite index reaches its maximum value when all available leading indicators issue warning signals. Therefore, for all composite indexes, the minimum value is 0 when no single indicator issues a warning signal. The maximum possible value is 100.

Predicting Crises

Composite indexes are used for predicting crisis probabilities. This can be done by dividing all sample observations into several groups, each

[6] This criticism, however, applies to any aggregate index, such as the Human Development Index or composite leading indicators of business cycles.

corresponding to a particular range of a composite index, and calculating the proportion of precrisis months (those falling within crisis windows) for each group, using the formula

$$P(C|I^l < I_t < I^u) = \frac{\text{no. of months with } I^l < I_t < I^u \text{ and falling within crisis windows}}{\text{total no. of months with } I^l < I_t < I^u} \quad (4.9)$$

where I_t is the value of the composite index at time t, I^l is the lower bound of a particular range of the composite index, I^u is the upper bound of the range, and $P\,(C|I^l < I_t < I^u)$ is the probability of a crisis occurring within 24 months if I_t lies in the range between I^l and I^u. In model estimation, we divide the entire sample, ranked by the value of each composite index, into five groups. The first contains all observations with the composite index equal to 0. The next four groups contain all the observations with the composite index greater than 0 and classified in percentiles into 0–25, 25–50, 50–75, 75–100 ranges for the currency crisis model; and into 0–50, 50–90, 90–95, and 95–100 ranges for the banking crisis model.

Using Equation 4.9, a crisis probability table can be constructed for each composite index. The probability table enables one to assign a particular level of crisis probability to each observed value of a composite index. For a composite index to issue warning signals, we need to choose a cutoff probability. A composite index will issue a warning signal in a particular month when its estimated crisis probability exceeds the cutoff level. The selection of cutoff probabilities involves trade-offs between Type-I and Type-II errors, as discussed earlier. But as a general rule, cutoff probabilities should be higher than the unconditional crisis probability as given by Equation 4.5.

4.3 A Currency Crisis EWS Model

Using monthly data[7] of six East Asian countries—Indonesia, Korea, Malaysia, Philippines, Singapore, and Thailand—from 1970 to 1995, a signaling approach-based currency crisis EWS model is constructed. Limiting the sample period through 1995 in model estimation allows us to test whether the model would have predicted the 1997 Asian financial crisis, by using data for 1996 and 1997 as out-of-sample. Our results are also compared, whenever possible, with those of two previous studies: Goldstein, Kaminsky, and Reinhart (2000), henceforth GKR, and Edison (2000), henceforth Edison.

[7] Several variables only have annual observations.

Crisis Episodes

Table 4.3 reports country-specific cutoff levels of monthly currency depreciation for identifying currency crisis episodes estimated using Equation 4.1. The cutoff levels have been converted and refer to declines in the US dollar value of a domestic currency. The estimated cutoff level during the sample period of 1970–1995 is 8.8% for Indonesia, 4% for Korea, 3% for Malaysia, 7.8% for Philippines, 2.7% for Singapore, and 2.5% for Thailand.

Table 4.3 **Cutoff Levels of Monthly Currency Depreciation, 1970–1995**

Country	**Cutoff Level** (%)
Indonesia	8.8
Korea	4.0
Malaysia	3.0
Philippines	7.8
Singapore	2.7
Thailand	2.5

Note: Cutoff levels refer to declines in the dollar value per unit of domestic currency.
Source: Author's estimates.

Using these cutoff levels, 28 currency crisis episodes are identified during 1970–1995 in the six countries, as reported in Table 4.4. Indonesia had five episodes, with currency depreciation ranging from 9% in August 1971 to 34% in November 1978; Korea had three, ranging from 12% in June 1971 to 17.6% in December 1974; Malaysia had seven, ranging from 3.5% in February 1985 to 7.6% in July 1975; the Philippines had five, ranging from 8% in November 1990 to 31.8% in February 1970; Singapore had six, ranging from 3.4% in March 1991 to 7.4% in July 1975; and Thailand had two, 8.7% in July 1981 and 15% in November 1984.

Therefore, across the six countries, exchange rates were on average more volatile in Indonesia, Korea, and Philippines than in Malaysia, Singapore, and Thailand. In fact, no depreciation instances in Malaysia and Singapore would have been classified as crisis episodes using the threshold for Indonesia or the Philippines.

It is worth noting that depreciation instances in Table 4.4 are considered crisis episodes purely based on the technical definition adopted in this study. In practice, some depreciation instances might have significant impact on the real sector and the entire economy, especially if they were accompanied

Table 4.4 **Episodes of Currency Crises in East Asia, 1970–1995**

Country	This Study[a]	GKR	Edison
Indonesia	Apr 1970 (13.8)	—	—
	Aug 1971 (8.9)	—	—
	Nov 1978 (33.6)	Nov 1978	Nov 1978
	Apr 1983 (27.4)	Apr 1983	Apr 1983
	Sep 1986 (30.7)	Sep 1986	Sep 1986
Korea	Jun 1971 (12.0)	Jun 1971	Jun 1971
	Dec 1974 (17.6)	Dec 1974	Dec 1974
	Jan 1980 (16.6)	Jan 1980	Jan 1980
Malaysia	Nov 1973 (4.9)	—	Nov 1973
	Jul 1975 (7.6)	Jul 1975	—
	Nov 1978 (4.4)	—	Nov 1978
	Mar 1980 (4.1)	—	Mar 1980
	Feb 1985 (3.5)	—	Feb 1985
	Mar 1986 (3.7)	—	—
	Dec 1993 (5.3)	—	Dec 1993
Philippines	Feb 1970 (31.8)	Feb 1970	—
	Jun 1983 (8.3)	Oct 1983	Oct 1983
	Oct 1984 (22.2)	Jun 1984	Jun 1984
	Feb 1986 (13.1)	—	Feb 1986
	Nov 1990 (8.0)	—	—
Singapore	—	—	Dec 1970
	Aug 1973 (3.8)	—	—
	Jul 1975 (7.3)	—	Jul 1975
	Nov 1978 (4.1)	—	Nov 1978
	Mar 1980 (4.4)	—	Mar 1980
	Aug 1985 (3.5)	—	—
	Mar 1991 (3.4)	—	—
Thailand	—	Nov 1978	Nov 1978
	Jul 1981 (8.7)	Jul 1981	Jul 1981
	Nov 1984 (15.0)	Nov 1984	Nov 1984

— = not defined as a crisis episode by the concerned study.

[a] Figures in parentheses are actual percentages of declines in the US dollar value per unit of domestic currency.

Sources: Author's estimates; Goldstein, Kaminsky, and Reinhart (2000); Edison (2000).

by banking crises. These episodes were "true crises" in a more conventional sense. On the other hand, some episodes, even if involving the same extent of depreciation as true crises, might have only limited impact, and not have been considered as crises at the time they occurred. In this study, we have not made any distinction between these two types of crisis episodes.

Some depreciation instances are not identified as crisis episodes even though they exceed their respective thresholds. This is because they occurred within 12 months of a previous crisis episode and, according to a commonly used rule, are considered as part of the previous crisis. During 1970–1995, there was one such instance each in Korea (October 1980), Malaysia (February 1981), and Singapore (November 1973), while there were four in the Philippines (September 1983, October 1983, June 1984, and February 1985).

Table 4.4 also compares crisis episodes identified in this study with those by GKR and Edison. In GKR and Edison, a particular month is classified as a crisis episode when the weighted average of the rates of month-on-month movements in the exchange rate and foreign reserves exceeds its sample mean by three standard deviations.[8] There are several months that are classified as crisis episodes by this study, but neither by GKR nor by Edison: in Indonesia, April 1970 (depreciation by 13.8%) and August 1971 (depreciation by 8.9%); in Malaysia, March 1986 (depreciation by 3.7%); in the Philippines, November 1990 (depreciation by 8%); and in Singapore, August 1973 (depreciation by 3.8%), August 1985 (depreciation by 3.5%), and March 1991 (depreciation by 3.4%). Meanwhile, two instances, November 1978 in Thailand and December 1970 in Singapore, were classified as crisis episodes by GKR and/or Edison, but not by this study. In GKR and Edison, the two were classified as unsuccessful attacks. November 1978 in Thailand involved reserve losses of 17.2% and 0.7% currency depreciation against the US dollar, and December 1970 in Singapore involved reserve losses of 12.4% and 0.6% currency depreciation. But a closer look at data suggests that the reserve losses in these two months were followed by large reserve gains in subsequent months, rather than lasting for consecutive months that one would expect if there were speculative attacks. Therefore, it does not appear justified to consider these as unsuccessful attacks.

Although the model identifies 28 currency crisis episodes, 4 episodes occurred in either 1970 or 1971, and hence have a crisis window of less than 24 months. These are not included in the model evaluation below.

[8] Despite using the same method, the two studies produced different results, especially in the case of Malaysia (Singapore was not included in GKR).

Selected Leading Indicators

Indicator selection in this study involves screening more than 60 economic and financial indicators collected from *International Financial Statistics* of the IMF and official national sources. From these, 40 are selected, each with an *NSR* of less than 1 at a chosen threshold, suggesting some predictive power. Table 4.5 lists the threshold in percentile and associated *NSR*, conditional crisis probability, number of crisis episodes predicted, and share of precrisis periods correctly called for each of the 40 leading indicators of the currency crisis model selected through the grid search procedure outlined in Section 4.2. The 24-month crisis window is used in obtaining these results. However, as part of sensitivity analyses, we also experimented with the 18-month and 12-month crisis windows, and found that most indicators' predictive performance deteriorates with shorter crisis windows.

Before looking at Table 4.5, it is important to note that the unconditional crisis probability of currency crises for the sample is 31%, meaning that if a particular month is randomly chosen from the sample data, there is a 31% probability that it falls within a crisis window and is associated with a currency crisis. For any leading indicator to be of predictive power, therefore, its conditional crisis probability at the chosen threshold should be greater than 31%. Key findings can be summarized as follows.

- All seven current account indicators screened have an *NSR* of less than 1, and therefore were selected. Among them, the real exchange rate, measured in deviations from its trend, performs the best.[9] It has a threshold in the 90th percentile, an *NSR* of 0.15, and a conditional crisis probability of 75%—meaning that when this indicator flashes a warning signal, there is a 75% probability that there would be a currency crisis within 24 months. This indicator predicts 10 of the 24 crisis episodes and correctly calls 20% of the precrisis periods in the sample.
- Of the 20 capital account indicators screened, 13 were selected.[10] The best performing is the ratio of short-term external debt to foreign reserves. It has a threshold in the 88th percentile, an *NSR* of 0.23, and a conditional crisis probability of 64%. It correctly calls 20% of the precrisis periods in the sample, but only predicts 6 of the 24 crisis episodes.

---

[9] A stochastic trend, estimated using the HP filter from 1970–1995 sample data, was used in computing deviations of the real exchange rate from its trend. The smoothing parameter of the HP filter was chosen such that the real exchange rate variable has the same level of *NSR* as when using a linear time trend.

[10] The eliminated capital account indicators are the ratio and 12-month change in the ratio of FDI to GDP, ratio of short-term capital flows to GDP, ratio and 12-month change in the ratio of total external debt to reserves, and ratio and 12-month change in the ratio of portfolio capital flows to GDP.

Table 4.5 **Leading Indicators of Currency Crises, 1970–1995**

Leading Indicator	**Threshold** (percentile)	**Noise-to-Signal Ratio**	**Conditional Crisis Probability** (%)	**No. of Crisis Episodes Predicted** (signaling at least once)	**Share of Precrisis Periods Correctly Called**[a] (%)	**No. of Crises during Sample Period**[b]
Current Account						
Real exchange rate against US$, deviation from trend[c]	90	0.15	75	10	20	24
Current account balance/GDI	18	0.45	50	13	26	18
Imports, 12-month % change	90	0.55	45	14	14	24
Trade account balance/GDP, 12-month change	11	0.69	40	17	14	24
Trade account balance/GDP	20	0.75	38	18	22	24
Exports, 12-month % change	11	0.78	37	13	13	24
Current account balance/GDI, 12-month change	14	0.87	34	7	12	17
Capital Account						
Short-term external debt/foreign reserves	88	0.23	64	6	20	19
Deposits in BIS banks/foreign reserves	89	0.36	54	6	13	13
M2/foreign reserves	90	0.40	53	11	16	24
Short-term capital flows/GDP, 12-month change	10	0.40	50	8	12	19
Foreign liabilities/foreign assets	90	0.43	52	9	12	24
Short-term external debt/foreign reserves, 12-month change	84	0.45	47	14	22	19
Foreign reserves, 12-month % change in months of imports covered	14	0.52	47	9	20	24
Deposits in BIS banks/foreign reserves, 12-month change	81	0.53	42	13	28	11
Foreign reserves, months of imports covered	19	0.58	44	14	28	24
M2/foreign reserves, 12-month change	85	0.68	40	14	19	24
Foreign liabilities/foreign assets, 12-month change	90	0.74	38	10	11	24
Domestic real interest rate differential from the US rate	90	0.75	36	14	12	16
Foreign reserves, 12-month % change	20	0.84	35	17	23	24

Financial Sector						
Real commercial bank deposits, 12-month % change	10	0.47	49	11	15	24
Lending-deposit rate spread	90	0.57	40	9	11	14
Lending-deposit rate spread, 12-month change	89	0.60	39	18	14	12
Deposits/M2, 12-month change	14	0.62	43	17	17	24
Deposits/M2	10	0.66	41	5	11	24
Real interest rate, 12-month change	80	0.60	39	20	29	12
Real interest rate	89	0.66	36	10	15	14
Loans/deposits, 12-month change	80	0.74	38	20	23	24
Loans/deposits	90	0.76	38	6	11	24
M1/GDP	86	0.76	38	10	15	24
Domestic credit/GDP	90	0.94	33	4	6	24
Real Sector						
CPI, 12-month % change	90	0.57	45	8	14	24
Stock prices in US$, 12-month % change	14	0.78	32	14	18	12
Fiscal Sector						
Central bank credit to public sector/GDP	90	0.71	36	7	11	18
Government consumption/GDP	80	0.75	38	11	23	24
Fiscal balance/GDP	20	0.76	38	14	25	24
Global Economy						
Oil price in US$, 12-month % change	90	0.52	47	9	15	24
Real US$/yen exchange rate, deviation from trend	11	0.53	46	12	14	24
US real interest rate	89	0.56	45	10	16	24
US annual growth rate	12	0.64	42	7	11	24

BIS = Bank for International Settlements, CPI = consumer price index, GDI = gross domestic investment, GDP = gross domestic product, M1 = narrow money, M2 = broad money.

[a] Number of precrisis periods predicted by the specified leading indicator as a percentage of total precrisis periods. Total precrisis periods equal the sum of all periods falling within crisis windows, that is, *A+C*, as defined in Table 4.2.

[b] Although the model identified 28 currency crisis episodes during 1970–1995, 4 episodes occurred either in 1970 or 1971, and hence have a crisis window of less than 24 months. These were not included in counting the crisis episodes. Differences in the number of crisis episodes during the sample period across leading indicators reflect differences in the length of their respective sample periods due to data availability.

[c] An increase denotes a real appreciation.

Source: Author's estimates.

- Eleven of the 15 financial sector indicators screened were selected.[11] The best performing is the 12-month percentage change in real commercial bank deposits.
- We screened four real sector indicators and selected two.[12] Between the two, the better performing is the 12-month growth of consumer prices.
- Among the eight fiscal sector indicators, three were selected.[13] The best performing is the central bank credit to the public sector/GDP ratio.
- Finally, of the seven global economy indicators screened, four were selected.[14] The best performing is the 12-month growth in the world oil price.

All the selected leading indicators are listed in Table 4.5 by category in order of performance as measured by *NSR*.

Although a leading indicator's threshold is uniform for the sample countries in percentile, it is country-specific in actual value. In some cases, differences in the actual threshold values (not reported here) are small across sample countries. Notable examples are the ratio and 12-month change in the ratio of current account balance to GDI, import growth, ratio and 12-month change in the ratio of trade balance to GDP, ratio and 12-month change in the ratio of foreign liabilities to foreign assets of the banking sector, ratio and 12-month change in the ratio of bank loans to bank deposits, lending-deposit interest rate spread, ratio of M1 to GDP, ratio of domestic credit to GDP, 12-month growth of stock prices, ratio of fiscal balance to GDP, and ratio of government consumption to GDP. For example, the threshold value of the current account balance/GDI ratio is -0.16 for Indonesia; -0.12 for Korea; and around -0.22 for Malaysia, Philippines, Singapore, and Thailand. In some other cases, however, differences are

[11] The eliminated financial sector indicators are the M2 multiplier, 12-month growth of the M2 multiplier, 12-month change in the ratio of domestic credit to GDP, and deviation of real M1 balance from its trend.

[12] The eliminated real sector indicators are the 12-month industrial growth and 12-month growth of stock prices in local currency.

[13] The eliminated fiscal indicators are the 12-month change in the central bank credit to the public sector/GDP ratio, 12-month change in the ratio of fiscal balance to GDP, 12-month change in the ratio of government consumption to GDP, and the ratio and 12-month change in the ratio of net credit to the public sector/GDP.

[14] The eliminated global economy indicators are the 12-month change in the US real interest rate, world oil price in US dollars, and the US quarter-on-quarter GDP growth.

quite significant. In the case of the short-term external debt/foreign reserves ratio, the threshold is 1.97 for Indonesia, 4.43 for Korea, 0.55 for Malaysia, 12.76 for the Philippines, 6.24 for Singapore, and 1.85 for Thailand. The threshold of the M2/foreign reserves ratio is more than 13 for Korea and the Philippines, about 10 for Thailand, 6.7 for Indonesia, 4.2 for Malaysia, and 1.3 for Singapore. Overall, it appears that actual threshold values are more divergent for capital account and financial sector indicators than for current account, fiscal sector, and real sector indicators.

How different are these results from those reported in GKR and Edison? Table 4.6 shows the threshold in percentile, *NSR*, conditional crisis probability, and share of crisis episodes predicted for each leading indicator analyzed in the two studies.

Comparing Table 4.6 with Table 4.5, it appears that, in general, results of this study are better. In both GKR and Edison, the real exchange rate is the best performing indicator. In GKR, it has a threshold in the 90th percentile, an *NSR* of 0.22, a conditional crisis probability of 62%, and a 58% share of crisis episodes predicted at least once (50 out of a total of 87). Results in Edison are not as good. In this study, the real exchange rate has the same threshold level, but a much lower *NSR* (0.15), and higher conditional crisis probability (75%), although a lower share of crisis episodes predicted (42%, that is, 10 out of a total of 24).

In both GKR and Edison, the real exchange rate is the only indicator with a conditional crisis probability above 50%. In this study, in addition to the real exchange rate, six other leading indicators each has a conditional crisis probability at 50% or above, including the ratio of current account balance to GDI, ratio of short-term external debt to foreign reserves, ratio of deposits in Bank for International Settlements (BIS) banks to foreign reserves, ratio of M2 to foreign reserves, 12-month change in the ratio of short-term capital flows to GDP, and ratio of foreign liabilities to foreign assets of the banking sector. To some extent, these differences could be a result of discrepancies in data coverage, variable definitions, and estimation procedures. But it is also possible that the leading indicators in this study perform better because of the focus on a smaller set of more homogenous countries.

Another notable difference between this study and GKR is the location of the threshold for the ratio of short-term capital flows to GDP. This indicator has a right-tail threshold in GKR (Edison did not use this indicator) while a left-tail threshold in this study. Theoretically, if the indicator is used as a proxy for the burden of short-term external liabilities, it should have a right-tail threshold as in GKR (the higher short-term external liabilities lead to higher vulnerability). But this indicator can also be interpreted as a proxy for foreign investor sentiment and, if that is the case, it should have a left-tail

Table 4.6 **Leading Indicators of Currency Crises in the GKR and Edison Studies**

Leading Indicator
Real exchange rate[b]
Current account balance/GDP
Stock price index
Current account balance/investment
Exports, 12-month % change
M2/foreign reserves
Excess real M1 balances
Real output
Overall fiscal balance/GDP
Foreign reserves
M2 multiplier
Short-term capital inflows/GDP
Domestic credit/GDP
General government consumption/GDP
Terms of trade
Real interest rate
Imports
Net credit to the public sector/GDP
Central bank credit to the public sector/GDP
Interest rate differential from US
Foreign direct investment/GDP
Bank deposits
Lending-deposit interest rate spread
US real output, 12-month % change
G-7 real output, 12-month % change
US interest rate, 12-month % change
Oil prices, 12-month % change
M2/foreign reserves
Short-term debt/foreign reserves, 12-month % change
Short-term debt/foreign reserves

G-7 = The Group of 7, GDP = gross domestic product, M1 = narrow money, M2 = broad money.

— = not used in the concerned study.

[a] Number of crisis episodes predicted by the specified leading indicator by flashing at least once as a percentage of total crisis episodes in the sample.

[b] An increase denotes a real depreciation.

Sources: Goldstein, Kaminsky, and Reinhart (2000) and Edison (2000).

GKR				Edison			
Threshold (percentile)	**Noise-to-Signal Ratio**	**No. of Crisis Episodes Predicted**[a] (%)	**Conditional Crisis Probability** (%)	**Threshold** (percentile)	**Noise-to-Signal Ratio**	**No. of Crisis Episodes Predicted**[a] (%)	**Conditional Crisis Probability** (%)
10	0.22	58	62.1	10	0.26	44	53
20	0.41	56	43.2	—	—	—	—
15	0.46	66	47.6	20	0.57	63	28
15	0.49	31	39.0	—	—	—	—
10	0.51	80	42.4	10	0.60	72	33
90	0.51	75	42.3	90	0.52	61	34
89	0.57	27	40.1	89	0.55	52	25
10	0.57	71	43.0	14	0.59	68	34
10	0.58	22	36.4	—	—	—	—
10	0.58	72	38.9	10	0.53	66	36
89	0.59	72	39.2	85	0.86	63	24
85	0.59	29	35.2	—	—	—	—
88	0.68	57	35.6	80	0.75	67	25
90	0.74	15	29.4	—	—	—	—
10	0.74	77	35.4	—	—	—	—
88	0.77	89	32.0	80	0.66	53	26
90	0.87	59	30.1	90	0.88	52	25
88	0.88	20	26.2	—	—	—	—
90	0.99	13	23.8	—	—	—	—
89	1.00	86	26.1	90	1.00	26	19
16	1.00	24	21.7	—	—	—	—
15	1.32	43	22.3	10	0.94	35	21
88	1.32	63	24.4	80	2.70	28	6
—	—	—	—	10	0.58	45	33
—	—	—	—	10	0.58	36	33
—	—	—	—	90	0.97	37	23
—	—	—	—	90	0.99	28	23
—	—	—	—	88	0.47	50	36
—	—	—	—	88	0.40	92	15
—	—	—	—	88	0.47	57	13

threshold (a sharp decline in short-term capital flows may signal a deterioration in investor sentiment and increasing vulnerability). In this study, the ratio of short-term external debt (a stock variable) to foreign reserves is used as a direct measure of the short-term external debt burden, and found to have a right-tail threshold. The threshold of the ratio of short-term capital flows to GDP is estimated at both tails, and found to work only at the left tail. Therefore, we interpret it as a proxy for foreign investor sentiment.

Composite Indexes and Crisis Probabilities

The two general composite indexes are constructed from the 40 selected leading indicators. Each sector composite index is constructed using all the selected leading indicators for each respective sector. For many indicators, both forms—the level and 12-month change (or percentage change) in the level—are found to have predictive power, and hence are included in constructing composite indexes as two separate indicators.[15]

One way to evaluate how useful composite indexes are in predicting currency crises in the sample is to look at whether crisis probability increases when the value of these indexes increases. Table 4.7 shows the crisis probabilities associated with various ranges of values for the eight composite indexes.

Between the two general composite indexes, the weighted Composite I outperforms the unweighted Composite II. The crisis probability is low, at 16%, when no leading indicator flashes. As the value of the index increases, the probability rises. The highest probability is 60% for the range of 18.2–100. These numbers compare very favorably with the unconditional crisis probability of 31% for currency crises in the sample, suggesting that Composite I has significant predictive power. Composite II, which is a simple sum of binary values of the 40 selected leading indicators, performs slightly worse. But crisis probabilities at various ranges suggest that it also has significant predictive power.

---

[15] We consider this the representative model. Two alternative models were also tested as part of sensitivity analysis. The first treats the level and 12-month change (or percentage change) in the level of the same indicator as one indicator in constructing composite indexes. This is done by aggregating two specifications of the same indicator—after being converted into a binary variable—before using it to construct composite indexes. The second uses only one specification for each indicator, either the level or 12-month change (or percentage change) in the level, depending on their relative predictive power. The two alternative models were found to underperform the representative model and hence are not reported here.

Table 4.7 **Composite Indexes and Probabilities of Currency Crises, 1970–1995**

Percentile	Range	*P*(%)	*N*	Range	*P*(%)	*N*
	Composite I			**Composite II**		
	$I = 0$	15.79	152	$I = 0$	15.79	152
0–25	$0 < I \leq 5.2$	12.82	429	$0 < I \leq 6.5$	14.69	429
25–50	$5.2 < I \leq 10.2$	23.49	430	$6.5 < I \leq 11.8$	28.14	430
50–75	$10.2 < I \leq 18.2$	30.54	430	$11.8 < I \leq 17.9$	29.07	430
75–100	$18.2 < I \leq 100$	60.33	431	$17.9 < I \leq 100$	54.29	431
	Current Account			**Capital Account**		
	$I = 0$	23.12	1008	$I = 0$	22.51	813
0–25	$0 < I \leq 9.2$	19.07	215	$0 < I \leq 8.5$	16.29	264
25–50	$9.2 < I \leq 16.6$	32.41	216	$8.5 < I \leq 15.1$	27.17	265
50–75	$16.6 < I \leq 31.5$	37.96	216	$15.1 < I \leq 28.6$	40.76	265
75–100	$31.5 < I \leq 100$	64.98	217	$28.6 < I \leq 100$	60.76	265
	Financial Sector			**Real Sector**		
	$I = 0$	25.80	717	$I = 0$	28.90	1502
0–25	$0 < I \leq 10.5$	19.44	288	$0 < I \leq 42.1$	18.92	74
25–50	$10.5 < I \leq 17.0$	33.91	289	$42.1 < I \leq 58.0$	25.68	74
50–75	$17.0 < I \leq 27.4$	32.18	289	$58.0 < I < 100$	33.33	75
75–100	$27.4 < I \leq 100$	46.71	289	$I = 100$	66.67	75
	Fiscal Sector			**Global Economy**		
	$I = 0$	25.51	1235	$I = 0$	25.65	1146
0–25	$0 < I \leq 32.9$	41.51	159	$0 < I \leq 11.5$	13.81	181
25–50	$32.9 < I \leq 34.8$	39.62	159	$11.5 < I \leq 29.7$	44.20	181
50–75	$34.8 < I \leq 65.3$	47.80	159	$29.7 < I \leq 30.6$	47.80	182
75–100	$65.3 < I \leq 100$	29.38	160	$30.6 < I \leq 100$	44.51	182

Range = range of composite index value
P = crisis probability
N = number of sample observations in each range
I = composite index value
Source: Author's estimates.

Table 4.7 also shows results for sector composite indexes.

The current account composite index outperforms all others. The crisis probability is low at about 23% when no leading indicator flashes. The highest probability is 65% when the value of this index ranges from 31.5 to 100. The results of the capital account, financial sector, and real sector composite indexes are also good. But the fiscal sector and global economy composite indexes do not perform as well. Although the crisis probability is on average higher when leading indicators issue warning signals than when no indicator flashes, the pattern of the crisis probability is not clear-cut. This suggests that, standing alone, the fiscal sector and global composite indexes do not have significant predictive power. Nevertheless, when the general composite indexes flash, they could be useful in helping identify sources of vulnerabilities.

To further evaluate performance of various composite indexes in the sample, we look at the number of crisis episodes predicted, precrisis periods correctly called as a share of total precrisis periods, and false alarms as a share of total warning signals, as reported in Table 4.8. We look at these measures at cutoff probabilities of 45% and 60%. And for comparison, we also report results at the 30% cutoff probability.[16]

Results in Table 4.8 are generally consistent with those in Table 4.7. By predicting up to 18 of the 24 crisis episodes included in the evaluation, and correctly calling 46% of the precrisis periods at a cutoff probability as high as 60% for Composite I, the performance of the model should be considered very satisfactory. Between the two general composite indexes, Composite I outperforms Composite II by all measures at both the 45% and 60% cutoff probabilities. Among the sector composite indexes, the current account and capital account composite indexes outperform the others, with the performance of the current account composite index being particularly impressive. In fact, at both the 45% and 60% cutoff probabilities, the current account composite index has a lower *NSR* and a lower percentage of false alarms than the two general composite indexes, although it predicts less crisis episodes and correctly calls less precrisis periods than the latter two. The real sector composite index has a lower *NSR* and a lower percentage of false alarms compared with the other sector composite indexes, with the exception of the current account, at both the 45% and 60% cutoff probabilities. But it only captures two crisis episodes and correctly calls 3.1% of the precrisis periods, far less than other sector composite indexes. This suggests that most currency crises in the sample countries during the sample period were not caused by the real sector problems alone, but when this index does issue warning signals, the signals are generally quite reliable.

Overall, we may classify the eight composite indexes into three groups according to their predictive power: strong performers including Composite I, Composite II, the current account composite index, and the capital account composite index; fair performers including the financial sector and real sector composite indexes; and weaker performers including the fiscal sector and global economy composite indexes.

---

[16] This is not recommended for the currency crisis model as the unconditional crisis probability for the sample is 31%.

Table 4.8 **Currency Crisis Model: In-Sample Evaluation**

	Composite I	Composite II	Current Account	Capital Account	Financial Sector	Real Sector	Fiscal Sector	Global Economy
Cutoff Probability of 60%								
NSR [[*B*/(*B*+*D*)]/[*A*/(*A*+*C*)]]	0.2915	—	0.2065	0.2956	—	0.2446	—	—
Number of crises predicted	18	0	15	14	0	2	0	0
% of precrisis periods correctly called [*A*/(*A*+*C*)]	46.0	0.0	24.1	29.4	0.0	3.1	0.0	0.0
% of false alarms [1-*A*/(*A*+*B*)]	38.7	—	30.9	39.0	—	34.6	—	—
Cutoff Probability of 45%								
NSR [[*B*/(*B*+*D*)]/[*A*/(*A*+*C*)]]	0.2915	0.3773	0.2065	0.2956	0.4377	0.2446	0.6458	0.5895
Number of crises predicted	18	18	15	14	21	2	8	6
% of precrisis periods correctly called [*A*/(*A*+*C*)]	46.0	41.8	24.1	29.4	24.3	3.1	15.1	5.3
% of false alarms [1-*A*/(*A*+*B*)]	38.7	45.0	30.9	39.0	48.6	34.6	58.3	56.1
Cutoff Probability of 30%								
NSR [[*B*/(*B*+*D*)]/[*A*/(*A*+*C*)]]	0.5275	0.3773	0.5465	0.4115	0.7138	0.3881	0.6112	0.5428
Number of crises predicted	23	18	20	17	21	8	19	19
% of precrisis periods correctly called [*A*/(*A*+*C*)]	68.2	41.8	50.9	48.4	56.9	13.7	40.7	41.8
% of false alarms [1-*A*/(*A*+*B*)]	53.3	45.0	54.2	47.1	60.7	45.7	56.9	54.0

— = undefined because *A* or *A*+*B* is zero.
Note: *A, B, C, D* are as defined in Table 4.2.
Source: Author's estimates.

Table 4.8 clearly shows the trade-offs between Type-I and Type-II errors. For example, at the 60% cutoff probability, Composite I predicts 18 crisis episodes, correctly calls 46% of the precrisis periods, and has a false alarm rate of 38.7%. In comparison, at the 30% cutoff probability it predicts 23 crisis episodes and correctly calls 68.2% of the precrisis periods, indicating lower Type-I errors; but at the same time, its false alarm rate rises to 53.3%, indicating higher Type-II errors. In policy analysis, a lower cutoff probability could be used if one is more concerned with missing crisis episodes, while a higher cutoff probability could be chosen if one is more concerned with the reliability of warning signals.

How different is the performance of these composite indexes compared with those in other studies? GKR and Edison did not report these measures for the composite indexes. However, Berg and Pattillo (1999) reproduced the results of the model reported in Kaminsky, Lizondo, and Reinhart (1998). They show that, at the 50% cutoff probability, the composite index, weighted by the inverses of *NSRs*, correctly called a mere 9% of the total precrisis periods and had a 30–44% false alarm rate in the sample. In comparison, the performance of the four strongly performing composite indexes in this study appears better.

Predicting Currency Crises in Sample

Table 4.9 reports the number of warning signals issued by each composite index within 24 months prior to each of the 24 currency crisis episodes during the 1970–1995 sample period at two cutoff probabilities, 45% and 60%.[17]

At both the 45% and 60% cutoff probabilities, Composite I predicts all the crisis episodes in Korea, Philippines, and Thailand, with an average number of warning signals per captured episode at 11.5, 14, and 22, respectively. In the case of Indonesia, it predicts 2 of the 3 crisis episodes, with an average number of warning signals per captured episode at 13.5. For Malaysia, it predicts 4 of the 7 crisis episodes, with an average of 13 signals per captured episode. And for Singapore, it predicts 4 of the 6 crisis episodes, with an average of 10.8 signals per captured episode. These numbers indicate a very high success rate for Composite I in predicting currency crises in the sample.

Composite II also has a high in-sample success rate at the 45% cutoff probability, although it issues fewer warning signals per captured crisis

[17] The four currency crisis episodes that occurred in either 1970 or 1971 are not considered, as their crisis windows are less than 24 months.

Table 4.9 **Warning Signals within 24 Months prior to Currency Crises, 1970–1995**

		Composite I		Composite II		Current Account		Capital Account		Financial Sector		Real Sector		Fiscal Sector		Global Economy	
Cutoff Probability (%)		**45**	**60**	**45**	**60**	**45**	**60**	**45**	**60**	**45**	**60**	**45**	**60**	**45**	**60**	**45**	**60**
Indonesia	Nov 1978	12	12	5	0	23	23	0	0	12	0	0	0	9	0	0	0
	Apr 1983	15	15	16	0	5	5	12	12	4	0	0	0	0	0	0	0
	Sep 1986	0	0	1	0	0	0	0	0	1	0	0	0	0	0	0	0
Korea	Dec 1974	8	8	8	0	3	3	5	5	7	0	0	0	0	0	0	0
	Jan 1980	15	15	14	0	18	18	0	0	1	0	0	0	0	0	7	0
Malaysia	Nov 1973	1	1	0	0	4	4	0	0	1	0	0	0	12	0	0	0
	Jul 1975	20	20	14	0	21	21	0	0	9	0	0	0	0	0	0	0
	Nov 1978	0	0	0	0	2	2	0	0	0	0	0	0	0	0	0	0
	Mar 1980	0	0	0	0	4	4	0	0	0	0	0	0	0	0	7	0
	Feb 1985	17	17	13	0	0	0	20	20	1	0	0	0	0	0	0	0
	Mar 1986	14	14	12	0	0	0	16	16	1	0	0	0	2	0	0	0
	Dec 1993	0	0	0	0	0	0	0	0	4	0	0	0	0	0	0	0
Philippines	Jun 1983	13	13	13	0	2	2	7	7	5	0	0	0	0	0	0	0
	Oct 1984	16	16	14	0	0	0	18	18	2	0	9	9	0	0	0	0
	Feb 1986	17	17	14	0	0	0	11	11	13	0	15	15	0	0	0	0
	Nov 1990	10	10	10	0	1	1	10	10	1	0	0	0	10	0	2	0
Singapore	Aug 1973	5	5	5	0	2	2	10	10	1	0	0	0	16	0	0	0
	Jul 1975	23	23	19	0	23	23	14	14	14	0	0	0	0	0	0	0
	Nov 1978	0	0	0	0	0	0	0	0	13	0	0	0	11	0	0	0
	Mar 1980	10	10	10	0	1	1	3	3	8	0	0	0	23	0	7	0
	Aug 1985	5	5	7	0	0	0	4	4	5	0	0	0	7	0	0	0
	Mar 1991	0	0	0	0	0	0	0	0	0	0	0	0	0	0	3	0
Thailand	Jul 1981	22	22	22	0	12	12	9	9	9	0	0	0	0	0	3	0
	Nov 1984	22	22	22	0	8	8	23	23	4	0	0	0	0	0	0	0

Source: Author's estimates.

episode than Composite I. However, it does not capture a single crisis episode at the 60% cutoff probability.

Among the sector composite indexes, the current account and capital account each predicts far more crisis episodes (15 and 14, respectively) and issues far more warning signals per captured episode (8.6 and 11.6, respectively) than the others at both the 45% and 60% cutoff probabilities. The real sector composite index captures two crisis episodes, with an average of 12 warning signals per captured crisis at both the 45% and 60% cutoff probabilities. All the other sector composite indexes only issue warning signals and predict crisis episodes at the cutoff probability of 45%.

4.4 A Banking Crisis EWS Model

The same data set used to estimate the currency crisis EWS model is used to estimate the banking crisis EWS model. The sample period is also limited to 1970–1995 for estimation.

Crisis Episodes

As discussed in Section 4.2, in this study we have not tried to identify banking crisis episodes from historical data or events. Instead, we rely on those identified by GKR, as listed in Table 4.10. Many empirical studies have documented banking crisis episodes for the sample countries we consider in this study. For instance, according to Lindgren, Garcia, and Saal (1996), Malaysia experienced a banking crisis during 1985–1988, the Philippines during 1981–1987, and Thailand during 1983–1987. Kaminsky and Reinhart (1999) identified banking crises in Indonesia in 1992, Malaysia in 1985, the Philippines in 1981, and Thailand in 1979 and 1983. Hardy and Pazarbasioglu (1998) differentiated between "crisis" and "distress" episodes. They detected distress episodes in Indonesia in 1992 and the Philippines in 1997, and a full-blown crisis in Indonesia and Korea in 1997, Malaysia in 1985, the Philippines in 1981, and Thailand in 1983 and 1997. Studies by Demirgüç-Kunt and Detragiache (1998a, 1998b, and 1999) noted banking crises in Indonesia in 1992–1994, Malaysia in 1985–1988, the Philippines in 1981–1987, and Thailand in 1983.

Most of these studies, however, were based on annual data and therefore did not indicate in which months these crisis episodes started. GKR is one of the few studies that provide such detail. According to GKR, during 1970–1995, there were two crisis episodes in Indonesia (November 1992 and January 1994), two in Korea (January 1983 and January 1986), one in Malaysia

Table 4.10 **Episodes of Banking Crises in East Asia, 1970–1997**

Country	IMF	Lindgren, Garcia, and Saal (1996)	Kaminsky and Reinhart (1999)	Hardy and Pazarbasioglu (1998)		Demirgüç-Kunt and Detragiache (1998a, 1998b, 1999)	Goldstein, Kaminsky, and Reinhart (2000)[b]
				Crisis	Distress		
Indonesia	1992		1992		1992	1992–1994	Nov 1992
							Jan 1994
	1997			1997			Jul 1997
Korea	1983						Jan 1983
							Jan 1986
	1997			1997			Jul 1997
Malaysia	1985	1985–1988	1985	1985		1985–1988	Jul 1985
							Sep 1997
Philippines	1981	1981–1987	1981	1981		1981–1987	Jan 1981
					1997		Jul 1997
Thailand			1979				Mar 1979
	1983	1983–1987	1983	1983		1983[a]	Jan 1983
							May 1996
	1997			1997			Jul 1997

[a] Included only in Demirgüç-Kunt and Detragiache (1999).
[b] The month indicates the starting date of each crisis.

(July 1985), one in the Philippines (January 1981), and two in Thailand (March 1979 and January 1983). In 1997 all five countries experienced a banking crisis. As noted by GKR, in most cases, the years identified as banking crisis episodes correspond with those found in other studies. However, there are several instances where the starting date is a year earlier than the others. Further, four crisis episodes identified by GKR were not documented in the other studies.

It has been suggested that currency crises are often accompanied by banking crises. Comparing Table 4.4 with Table 4.10 reveals that, apart from the 1997 episode that involved both currency and banking crises for all five crisis-affected countries, only one banking crisis episode occurred within a half year after a currency crisis. This was the July 1985 episode in Malaysia. The timing of other banking crisis episodes appears quite different from that of the currency crisis episodes.

Selected Leading Indicators

The same set of leading indicators screened for the currency crisis model is also tested for the banking crisis model. Table 4.11 reports the threshold, *NSR*, conditional crisis probability, number of crisis episodes predicted, and share of precrisis periods correctly called for each of the 40 individual leading indicators selected for the banking crisis model.

The unconditional crisis probability for the banking crisis EWS model is 10%, meaning that if a particular month is randomly chosen from the sample data, there is a 10% probability that this month is associated with a banking crisis. Again, for any leading indicator to have predictive power, its conditional probability at the chosen threshold should be greater than 10%.

- Of the seven current account indicators screened, only three were selected. The best performer is the ratio of the current account balance to GDI, with a threshold in the 11th percentile, an *NSR* of 0.50, and a conditional crisis probability of 24%. It predicts 4 of the 8 banking crisis episodes in the sample and correctly calls 17% of the precrisis periods. It is interesting to note that, unlike in the currency crisis EWS model, real appreciation of domestic currencies is not an important predictor of banking crises in the sample countries during 1970–1995.[18]

[18] The banking crisis model uses the JP Morgan real effective exchange rate, as the real exchange rate against the US dollar measured in deviations from its trend was found to have an *NSR* greater than 1.

- Of the 20 capital account indicators screened, 12 were chosen. The indicator that outperforms all others is the ratio of foreign liabilities to foreign assets of the banking sector. With a threshold in the 85th percentile, it has an *NSR* of 0.26 and a conditional crisis probability of 30%. It predicts 7 of the 8 crisis episodes and correctly calls 37% of the precrisis periods.
- Of the 14 financial sector indicators tested, 12 were selected. The 12-month change in the real domestic interest rate is the best performer. With a threshold in the 89th percentile, it has an *NSR* of 0.34 and a conditional crisis probability of 36%. The number of crisis episodes it predicts is 5 and share of the precrisis periods it correctly calls is 26%.
- Two of the four real sector indicators screened were chosen. With a threshold in the 14th percentile, the 12-month growth in stock prices in local currency has an *NSR* of 0.48 and a conditional crisis probability of 23%. It predicts 7 crisis episodes and correctly calls 26% of the precrisis periods.
- Six fiscal indicators were selected from the eight screened. The net credit to the public sector/GDP ratio performs best. With a threshold in the 80th percentile, it has an *NSR* of 0.39 and a conditional crisis probability of 22%. It predicts 6 crisis episodes and correctly calls 43% of the precrisis periods.
- Six global economic indicators were tested, with five selected. The best performing is the US real interest rate. With a threshold in the 88th percentile, it has an *NSR* of 0.30 and a conditional crisis probability of 27%. It predicts 5 crisis episodes and correctly calls 33% of the precrisis periods.

All selected indicators are listed in Table 4.11 by category in order of performance measured by *NSR*.

There are clear differences when comparing the selected indicators for the banking crisis model (and their associated performance measures) with those of the currency crisis model.

First, leading indicators selected for the banking crisis model have in general less predictive power than those for the currency crisis model, suggesting that banking crises are more difficult to predict.

Second, across the six categories, as one would expect, current account indicators are far less useful in predicting banking crises than currency crises, while financial sector indicators are more important in predicting banking crises than currency crises.

Table 4.11 **Leading Indicators of Banking Crises, 1970–1995**

Leading Indicator	**Threshold** (percentile)	**Noise-to-Signal Ratio**	**Conditional Crisis Probability** (%)	**No. of Crisis Episodes Predicted** (signaling at least once)	**Share of Precrisis Periods Correctly Called**[a] (%)	**No. of Crises during Sample Period**
Current Account						
Current account balance/GDI	11	0.50	24	4	17	8
Real effective exchange rate, deviation from trend[b]	90	0.58	16	5	16	8
Exports, 12-month % change	20	0.79	13	7	26	8
Capital Account						
Foreign liabilities/foreign assets	85	0.26	30	7	37	8
Foreign reserves, months of imports covered	10	0.29	28	3	28	8
Short-term external debt/foreign reserves	80	0.33	28	5	50	8
Short-term capital flows/GDP, 12-month change	10	0.37	27	4	15	8
Deposits in BIS banks/foreign reserves	82	0.38	34	6	34	7
Short-term external debt/foreign reserves, 12-month change	90	0.41	25	3	17	8
Foreign liabilities/foreign assets, 12-month change	83	0.43	21	6	32	8
M2/foreign reserves	90	0.49	19	3	18	8
Deposits in BIS banks/foreign reserves, 12-month change	87	0.75	21	3	13	7
M2/foreign reserves, 12-month change	88	0.76	13	4	15	8
Domestic real interest rate differential from the US rate	80	0.80	17	5	26	8
Short-term capital flows/GDP	18	0.95	12	5	18	8
Financial Sector						
Real interest rate, 12-month change	89	0.34	36	5	26	7
M2 multiplier	81	0.43	21	4	30	8
Domestic credit/GDP	80	0.47	19	5	30	8

M2 multiplier, 12-month % change	82	0.49	19	8	31	8
Domestic credit/GDP, 12-month change	90	0.56	17	3	13	8
Real interest rate	88	0.56	26	5	20	8
Lending-deposit rate spread, 12-month change	90	0.68	21	4	12	6
Loans/deposits, 12-month change	80	0.69	15	6	26	8
Lending-deposit rate spread	82	0.70	22	4	22	8
Loans/deposits	88	0.70	14	3	15	8
Real commercial bank deposits, 12-month % change	20	0.82	13	7	23	8
Deposits/M2, 12-month change	20	0.83	12	6	22	8
Real Sector						
Stock prices in local currency, 12-month % change	14	0.48	23	7	26	6
Industrial production index, 12-month % change	15	0.84	13	8	18	5
Fiscal Sector						
Net credit to public sector/GDP	80	0.39	22	6	43	8
Central bank credit to public sector/GDP	90	0.48	22	2	15	8
Central bank credit to public sector/GDP, 12-month change	82	0.49	23	4	33	8
Government consumption/GDP	86	0.51	18	2	20	8
Fiscal balance/GDP	13	0.58	16	2	20	8
Net credit to public sector/GDP, 12-month change	88	0.59	17	3	14	8
Global Economy						
US real interest rate	88	0.30	27	5	33	8
Oil price in US$	86	0.38	23	3	33	8
US real interest rate, 12-month change	90	0.48	20	3	15	8
US annual growth rate	12	0.59	17	2	14	8
Real US$/yen exchange rate, deviation from trend	11	0.64	15	4	14	8

BIS = Bank for International Settlements, GDI = gross domestic investment, GDP = gross domestic product, M2 = broad money.

[a] Number of precrisis periods predicted by the specified leading indicator as a percentage of total precrisis periods. Total precrisis periods equal the sum of all periods falling within crisis windows, that is, *A+C*, as defined in Table 4.2.

[b] An increase denotes a real appreciation.

Source: Author's estimates.

Third, ranked by *NSR*, the top five leading indicators for the banking crisis model are the ratio of banking sector foreign liabilities to foreign assets, months of imports covered by foreign reserves, US real interest rate, ratio of short-term external debt to foreign reserves, and 12-month change in the domestic real interest rate. For the currency crisis EWS model, the top five indicators are the deviation of the real exchange rate against the US dollar from its trend, ratio of short-term external debt to foreign reserves, ratio of deposits in BIS banks to foreign reserves, ratio of M2 to foreign reserves, and 12-month change in the ratio of short-term capital flows to GDP.

Table 4.12 lists the leading indicators studied in GKR for the banking crisis model and their key performance measures. A comparison with this study (Table 4.11) reveals some differences. First, there are more leading indicators in this study than in GKR. Indicators used in this study but not in GKR include the ratio and 12-month change in the ratio of banking sector foreign liabilities to foreign assets, ratio and 12-month change in the ratio of short-term external debt to foreign reserves, ratio and 12-month change in the ratio of deposits in BIS banks to foreign reserves, ratio and 12-month change in the ratio of bank loans to deposits, world oil prices, and the real US dollar/yen exchange rate. Some of these additional indicators are found to have significant predictive power, for example, the ratio of foreign liabilities to foreign assets of the banking sector, our best performing indicator. Second, for indicators used in both studies, it appears that, overall, those used in this study have larger conditional crisis probabilities and, therefore, are more reliable. Third, for indicators used in both studies, the performance ranking is also different. In GKR, the top five indicators are the real exchange rate, ratio of short-term capital inflows to GDP, ratio of current account balance to GDI, stock prices, and M2 multiplier. None of these is among the top five indicators of the model developed in this study.

Examining country-specific threshold values of selected leading indicators for the banking crisis model shows that almost all the financial sector indicators have a more stringent threshold in the banking crisis EWS model (the threshold being closer to the mean) than in the currency crisis EWS model. This suggests that the banking crisis model is less tolerant to deterioration in financial sector indicators than the currency crisis model. Other indicators that have a more stringent threshold in the banking crisis model are the ratio and 12-month change in the ratio of foreign liabilities to foreign assets of the banking sector, ratio of short-term external debt to foreign reserves, ratio of deposits in BIS banks to foreign reserves, real interest rate differential from the US rate, US real interest rate, and 12-month growth of stock prices.

Table 4.12 **Leading Indicators of Banking Crises in the GKR Study**

Leading Indicator	**Noise-to-Signal Ratio**	**Share of Crisis Episodes Predicted** (signaling at least once, %)	**Conditional Crisis Probability** (%)
Real exchange rate	0.35	52	24.0
Short-term capital inflows/GDP	0.38	43	36.8
Current account balance/investment	0.38	38	36.1
Stock prices	0.46	76	23.4
M2 multiplier	0.46	63	18.3
Overall budget deficit/GDP	0.47	52	26.9
Current account balance/GDP	0.50	33	29.3
Central bank credit to the public sector/GDP	0.52	23	23.8
Real output	0.54	90	17.3
Exports	0.68	79	14.3
Real interest rate	0.68	96	16.8
Net credit to the public sector/GDP	0.72	15	18.3
Real interest rate differential	0.73	100	15.6
Bank deposits	0.73	64	12.9
M2/foreign reserves	0.84	72	11.4
Excess real M1 balances	0.88	44	11.0
Domestic credit/GDP	0.89	46	10.9
Foreign reserves	0.92	83	10.7
Terms of trade	1.01	92	11.6
Foreign direct investment/GDP	1.05	24	15.6
General government consumption/GDP	1.44	15	10.0
Lending-deposit interest rate spread	1.48	56	8.3
Imports	1.75	64	6.0

GDP = gross domestic product, M1 = narrow money, M2 = broad money.
Source: Goldstein, Kaminsky, and Reinhart (2000).

Composite Indexes and Crisis Probabilities

Two general and six sector composite indexes are also constructed for the banking crisis model. Table 4.13 reports crisis probabilities associated with various ranges of values for these composite indexes.

Between the two general composite indexes, Composite I, which is weighted by inverses of *NSRs*, outperforms Composite II. Both have a crisis probability of less than 2% when no indicator flashes. The maximum probability is 50% for Composite I, when its value reaches 35 and above, and 47.7% for Composite II, when its value reaches about 33 and above.

Table 4.13 **Composite Indexes and Probabilities of Banking Crises, 1970–1995**

Percentile	Range	*P* (%)	*N*	Range	*P* (%)	*N*
	Composite I			**Composite II**		
	$I = 0$	1.290	155	$I = 0$	1.290	155
0–50	$0 < I \le 10.9$	3.846	858	$0 < I \le 12.2$	4.196	858
50–90	$10.9 < I \le 28.0$	15.720	687	$12.2 < I \le 27.6$	16.449	687
90–95	$28.0 < I \le 35.3$	30.233	86	$27.6 < I \le 32.6$	23.256	86
95–100	$35.3 < I \le 100$	50.000	86	$32.6 < I \le 100$	47.674	86
	Current Account			**Capital Account**		
	$I = 0$	10.069	1301	$I = 0$	2.938	817
0–50	$0 < I \le 40.2$	16.491	285	$0 < I \le 20.7$	9.677	527
50–90	$40.2 < I \le 65.5$	10.965	228	$20.7 < I \le 42.6$	26.066	422
90–95	$65.5 < I \le 74.8$	24.138	29	$42.6 < I \le 50.5$	22.642	53
95–100	$74.8 < I \le 100$	6.897	29	$50.5 < I \le 100$	28.302	53
	Financial Sector			**Real Sector**		
	$I = 0$	3.763	558	$I = 0$	10.386	1088
0–50	$0 < I \le 19.7$	7.622	656	$0 < I \le 63.9$	20.290	138
50–90	$19.7 < I \le 35.2$	14.829	526	$63.9 < I < 100$	19.820	111
90–95	$35.2 < I \le 41.7$	39.394	66	} $I = 100$	10.715	28
95–100	$41.7 < I \le 100$	56.061	66			
	Fiscal Sector			**Global Economy**		
	$I = 0$	10.086	1160	$I = 0$	6.882	1206
0–50	$0 < I \le 30.7$	6.197	355	$0 < I \le 23.6$	13.253	332
50–90	$30.7 < I \le 64.8$	14.737	285	$23.6 < I \le 68.0$	25.094	267
90–95	$64.8 < I \le 69.4$	52.778	36	$68.0 < I \le 71.2$	27.273	33
95–100	$69.4 < I \le 100$	33.333	36	$71.2 < I \le 100$	26.471	34

Range = range of composite index value
P = crisis probability
N = number of sample observations in each range
I = composite index value
Source: Author's estimates.

The performance of the two general composite indexes is better than most sector composite indexes, with the exception of the financial sector composite index.

The financial sector composite index has a maximum crisis probability of 56%, higher than that for Composites I and II. But it also has a higher minimum crisis probability when no indicator flashes than do the two general composite indexes. Among the other five sector composite indexes, the capital account, fiscal sector, and global economy indexes also perform well. The crisis probability is only at 2.9% for the capital account index and 6.9% for the global economy index when no indicator flashes, but it rises to more than 25% when their values reach about 50 and above. For the fiscal sector index, the crisis probability is 10% when no indicator flashes, the same as the unconditional probability. But it rises to as high as 52% when more than half of the indicators issue warning signals. The current account and real sector composite indexes do not perform well in predicting banking crises.

To further evaluate the predictive power of these composite indexes, we calculate the number of crisis episodes predicted, precrisis periods correctly called as a percentage of total precrisis periods, and false alarms as a percentage of total warning signals, as reported in Table 4.14. Considering that the unconditional crisis probability is only 10% for the banking crises in the sample, we look at these measures at 30%, 40%, and 50% cutoff probabilities.

With eight banking crisis episodes in the sample, and the number of crisis episodes predicted reaching 6–7 at a cutoff probability of 30% and 3–4 at the cutoff probability of 40% or 50% for some composite indexes, the model could be considered having significant predictive power. Between the two general composite indexes, Composite I outperforms Composite II by all measures and at all cutoff probabilities. Among the sector-specific composite indexes, the financial sector index outperforms all others. In fact, the financial sector composite index predicts more crisis episodes than Composite I at all three cutoff probabilities, although it correctly calls a lower percentage of the precrisis periods, and has a slightly higher *NSR* compared with the latter at the 40% and 50% cutoff probabilities. The fiscal sector composite index has a smaller false alarm rate than the financial sector composite index, but it only predicts 1–2 crisis episodes and correctly calls 10–20% of the precrisis periods. Overall, the eight composite indexes can also be classified into three groups according to their predictive power shown in Table 4.14: strong performers including Composite I and the financial sector; fair performers including Composite II and the fiscal sector; and weaker performers including the current account, capital account, real sector, and global economy composite indexes.

Table 4.14 **Banking Crisis Model: In-Sample Evaluation**

	Composite I	Composite II	Current Account	Capital Account	Financial Sector	Real Sector	Fiscal Sector	Global Economy
Cutoff Probability of 30%								
NSR [[*B*/(*B*+*D*)]/[*A*/(*A*+*C*)]]	0.1676	0.1209	—	—	0.1372	—	0.1195	—
Number of crises predicted	6	3	0	0	7	0	2	0
% of precrisis periods correctly called [*A*/(*A*+*C*)]	39.4	22.3	0.0	0.0	25.7	0.0	17.7	0.0
% of false alarms [1-*A*/(*A*+*B*)]	59.9	51.9	—	—	55.0	—	51.6	—
Cutoff Probability of 40%								
NSR [[*B*/(*B*+*D*)]/[*A*/(*A*+*C*)]]	0.1096	0.1209	—	—	0.1283	—	0.1123	—
Number of crises predicted	3	3	0	0	4	0	1	0
% of precrisis periods correctly called [*A*/(*A*+*C*)]	24.6	22.3	0.0	0.0	12.0	0.0	10.9	0.0
% of false alarms [1-*A*/(*A*+*B*)]	49.4	51.9	—	—	53.3	—	50.0	—
Cutoff Probabiliy of 50%								
NSR [[*B*/(*B*+*D*)]/[*A*/(*A*+*C*)]]	0.1096	—	—	—	0.1283	—	0.1123	—
Number of crises predicted	3	0	0	0	4	0	1	0
% of precrisis periods correctly called [*A*/(*A*+*C*)]	24.6	0.0	0.0	0.0	12.0	0.0	10.9	0.0
% of false alarms [1-*A*/(*A*+*B*)]	49.4	—	—	—	53.3	—	50.0	—

— = undefined because *A* or *A*+*B* is zero.
Note: *A*, *B*, *C*, *D* are as defined in Table 4.2.
Source: Author's estimates.

Predicting Banking Crises in Sample

Table 4.15 reports the number of warning signals issued within 24 months prior to each banking crisis episode during the 1970–1995 sample period at two cutoff probabilities, 30% and 50%.

At the 30% cutoff probability, Composite I predicts all crisis episodes in Indonesia, Korea, and Malaysia, with an average number of signals per captured episode at about 10. It also predicts 1 of the 2 episodes in Thailand, with 22 warning signals. But it does not catch the crisis episode in the Philippines. At the higher 50% cutoff probability, it still manages to predict 3 of the 8 banking crisis episodes in the sample with an average number of signals per predicted crisis at about 14.

The performance of Composite II is not as good as Composite I. But at the 30% cutoff probability, it predicts 3 of the 8 crisis episodes with an average number of signals per captured episode at 13. At the 50% cutoff level, none of the crises is predicted by Composite II.

Among the sector composite indexes, the financial sector composite index has the best performance. At the 30% cutoff level, it predicts 7 out of the 8 crisis episodes with an average number of signals per captured episode of over 7. The only crisis it misses is the March 1979 episode in Thailand. At the higher 50% cutoff level, it still manages to predict 4 episodes with an average number of signals per captured crisis episode of about 6. The fiscal sector composite index predicts 2 crisis episodes at the 30% cutoff level, with an average number of signals per captured episode at about 15. And, at the 50% cutoff level, it also manages to predict 1 crisis with 19 signals. The current account, capital account, real sector, and global economy composite indexes issue no warning signals at either the 30% or 50% cutoff probability.

4.5 Predicting the 1997 Asian Financial Crisis—Out-of-Sample Evaluations

The real test of an EWS model's predictive ability is to examine its out-of-sample performance. We use data for 1996 and 1997 out of sample to ask the question—had the EWS developed in this study existed prior to the 1997 Asian crisis, could it have anticipated the event? We evaluate both currency and banking crisis models. In estimating deviations of the real exchange rate (for the currency crisis model) and real effective exchange rate (for the banking crisis model) from their respective stochastic long-term trends, we use data only up to the month preceding the 1997 crisis episode

Table 4.15 **Warning Signals within 24 Months prior to Banking Crises, 1970–1995**

		Composite I		Composite II		Current Account		Capital Account		Financial Sector		Real Sector		Fiscal Sector		Global Economy	
Cutoff Probability (%)		**30**	**50**	**30**	**50**	**30**	**50**	**30**	**50**	**30**	**50**	**30**	**50**	**30**	**50**	**30**	**50**
Indonesia	Nov 1992	4	0	0	0	0	0	0	0	13	9	0	0	0	0	0	0
	Jan 1994	4	0	0	0	0	0	0	0	11	5	0	0	0	0	0	0
Korea	Jan 1983	23	14	14	0	0	0	0	0	13	8	0	0	19	19	0	0
	Jan 1986	5	0	0	0	0	0	0	0	3	0	0	0	0	0	0	0
Malaysia	Jul 1985	15	9	7	0	0	0	0	0	4	1	0	0	0	0	0	0
Philippines	Jan 1981	0	0	0	0	0	0	0	0	1	0	0	0	0	0	0	0
Thailand	Mar 1979	0	0	0	0	0	0	0	0	0	0	0	0	0	0	0	0
	Jan 1983	22	20	18	0	0	0	0	0	5	0	0	0	12	0	0	0

Source: Author's estimates.

for each of the sample countries. This would ensure that the out-of-sample evaluations reflect *ex ante* forecasting.

Table 4.16 shows starting dates of the 1997 currency and banking crises in the six East Asian countries. For the starting dates of banking crises, we follow those identified in GKR. According to GKR, the 1997 banking crisis began in July in Indonesia, Korea, Philippines, and Thailand, and in September in Malaysia. There was no banking crisis in Singapore. Starting dates of currency crises are identified by using the cutoff levels of currency depreciation reported in Table 4.3. In each of the six countries reviewed, there were several instances when the percentage of depreciation exceeded respective cutoff levels. Because many of these instances occurred within 12 months, we consider them as part of the same crisis episode. According to this rule, Indonesia, Korea, Malaysia, Philippines, Singapore, and Thailand each had one currency crisis episode during 1996–1997, with the crisis starting in December, November, August, July, August, and July, in 1997, respectively.

Table 4.16 **Episodes of Currency and Banking Crises in East Asia, 1996–1997**

Country	Currency Crisis	Banking Crisis
Indonesia	Dec 1997	Jul 1997
Korea	Nov 1997	Jul 1997
Malaysia	Aug 1997	Sep 1997
Philippines	Jul 1997	Jul 1997
Singapore	Aug 1997	
Thailand		May 1996
	Jul 1997	Jul 1997

Sources: Author's estimates; Goldstein, Kaminsky, and Reinhart (2000).

The Currency Crisis EWS Model

CRISIS PROBABILITIES

Figures 4.1–4.6 plot the time series of crisis probabilities monthly from 1970 to 1997, estimated on the basis of Composite I, the better performing general composite index. As noted, crisis probabilities before 1996 are in-sample estimates and those for 1996 and 1997 are out-of-sample predictions. The specific dates indicate the starting dates of currency crises.

In Indonesia (Figure 4.1), the estimated crisis probability increases to 60% in December 1995, the first month of the 24-month window for the December 1997 crisis episode. But it falls to 30% in the second month, and remains at that level or below for the remaining months of the crisis window preceding the rupiah's 21.6% depreciation. Therefore, the model does not work in predicting the 1997 currency crisis episode in Indonesia. It is worth mentioning that GKR and Edison also fail to predict Indonesia's 1997 crisis.

In the case of Korea (Figure 4.2), the crisis probability remains below 25% or below for most months during 1990–1995. It begins climbing in January 1997, reaches 60% in July 1997, and remains at this level until November 1997, when the won depreciated by 17%.

In Malaysia (Figure 4.3), the crisis probability increases from 30% in December 1996 to 60% in January 1997, and stays at this level until the ringgit depreciated 11.1% in August 1997.

The Philippines (Figure 4.4) was less affected by the 1997 crisis. There have been suggestions that the Philippines' problems were caused more by "regional contagion" than its own weakness. However, our model clearly shows a buildup of financial vulnerability beginning in 1994. The crisis probability increases from 30% to 60% in early 1996, and stays at this level for 12 consecutive months before July 1997, when the peso depreciated by about 9%.

The model does not work well in the case of Singapore (Figure 4.5). The crisis probability increases prior to the 3.7% depreciation of the Singapore dollar in August 1997. But compared with other countries, the increase was much less pronounced.

Finally, in Thailand (Figure 4.6), after its 1984 episode, the crisis probability remains below 25% for many years. However, the crisis probability begins to rise in 1994, accelerates in 1995, and reaches 60% in 6 of the 12 months preceding the baht's 19.6% depreciation in July 1997.

As we have pointed out, this study uses a stochastic trend as a proxy for the equilibrium real exchange rate in estimating deviations from the trend of the real exchange rate. As part of sensitivity analysis, we also estimated two alternative currency crisis models: one assumes a commonly used deterministic trend for the real exchange rate and the other excludes the real exchange rate as a leading indicator. The results, reported in Appendix 4.1, suggest that the currency crisis EWS model assuming a linear trend for the real exchange rate performs similarly in predicting the 1997 currency crisis as the model assuming the stochastic trend described above, with the exception of the episode in Korea, which was predicted by the latter but not by the former (Figures 4.A.1–4.A.6). Although the model without the real exchange rate performs worse than the models with the real exchange rate variable, it issues warning signals during the 24 months preceding the 1997 currency crisis in Indonesia, Korea, Malaysia, and Thailand at a cutoff probability of over 50%, with the signals quite persistent for the latter two countries (Figures 4.A.7–4.A.12).

WARNING SIGNALS BY COMPOSITE INDEXES AND LEAD TIME

Table 4.17 reports the number of warning signals issued by various composite indexes and their lead time at the two cutoff probability levels, 45% and 60%. Composite I issues warning signals for all five sample countries seriously affected by the 1997 crisis at both cutoff levels. It issues 1 signal with a lead time of 24 months for Indonesia, 4 signals with a lead time of 4 months for Korea, 9 signals with a lead time of 24 months for Malaysia, 15 signals with a lead time of 22 months for the Philippines, and 13 signals with a lead time of 24 months for Thailand. But it issues no signals for Singapore. In comparison, Composite II only issues warning signals at the 45% cutoff probability. But it issues persistent signals in the case of Malaysia and Thailand, suggesting that it also has good predictive power.

Among the sector composite indexes, the current account composite index issues persistent signals for all the crisis-affected countries, with the exception of Indonesia, at both the 45% and 60% cutoff probabilities. Among other sector indexes, the capital account issues warning signals for Indonesia, Malaysia, and Thailand at both the 45% and 60% cutoff probabilities. The financial sector composite index also issues warning signals for the three countries, but only at the 45% cutoff probability. There are no warning signals from other sector composite indexes at either the 45% or 60% cutoff level.

WARNING SIGNALS BY INDIVIDUAL LEADING INDICATORS

Figures 4.7–4.12 plot the number of leading indicators signaling in each month during the entire 1970–1997 period. Again, those before 1996 are in-sample estimates, while those for 1996 and 1997 are out-of-sample predictions. As we can see, in most cases the number of signaling indicators increases when a crisis approaches, providing strong support for the usefulness of composite leading indexes. Prior to the 1997 crisis, the number

Figures 4.1–4.6 **Currency Crises and Crisis Probabilities Predicted by Composite I, 1970–1997**
Specific dates indicate crisis episodes

4.1 **Indonesia**

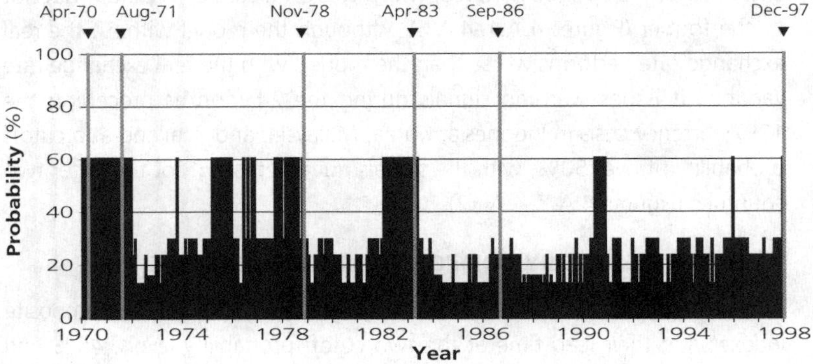

4.2 **Korea**

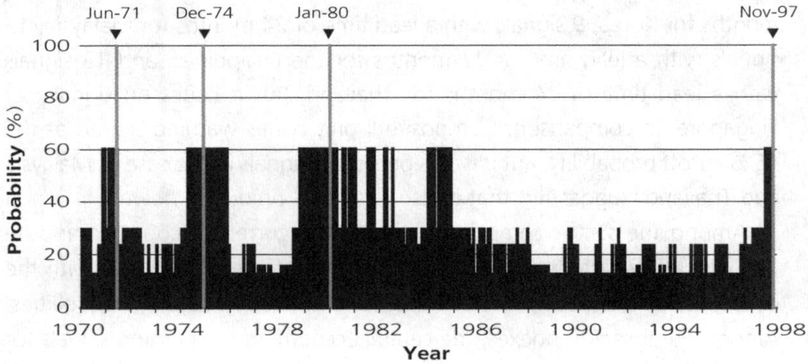

4.3 **Malaysia**

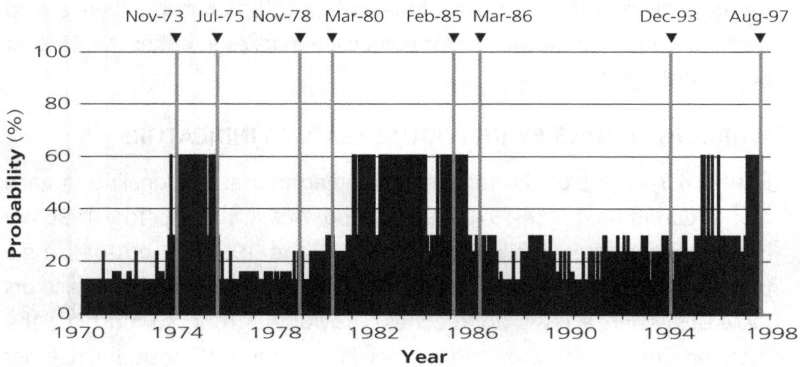

4.4 **Philippines**

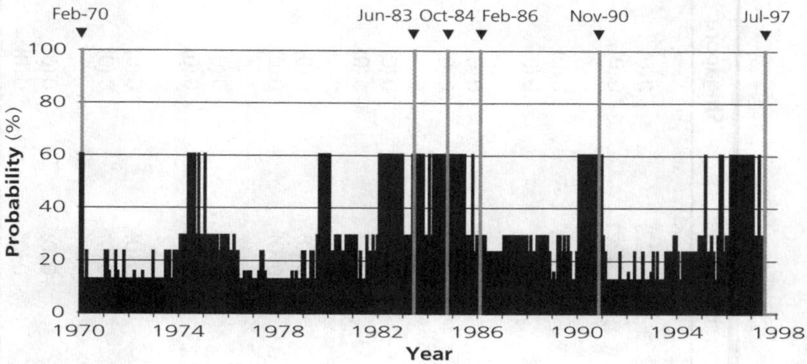

4.5 **Singapore**

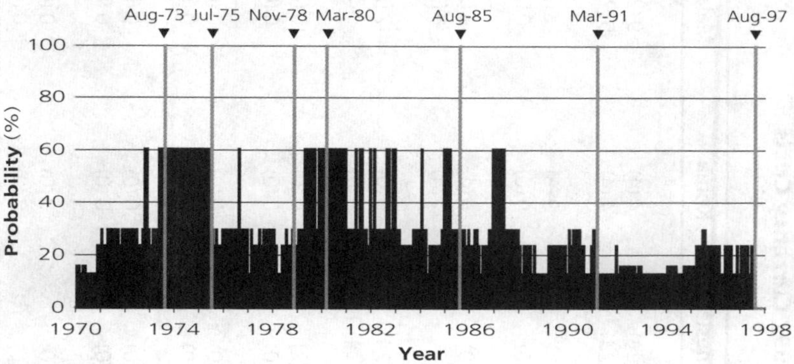

4.6 **Thailand**

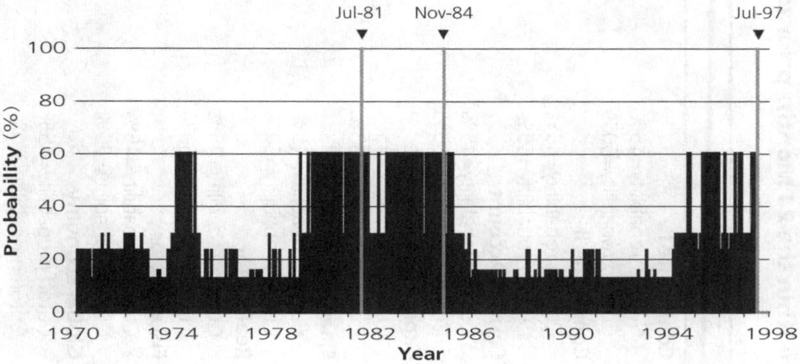

Table 4.17 **Number of Signals and Lead Time (in months) of Composite Indexes within the 24 Months prior to the 1997 Currency Crisis**

	Indonesia	Korea	Malaysia	Philippines	Singapore	Thailand
Composite I						
Cutoff probability=45%	1 (24)	4 (4)	9 (24)	15 (22)	0 (0)	13 (24)
Cutoff probability=60%	1 (24)	4 (4)	9 (24)	15 (22)	0 (0)	13 (24)
Composite II						
Cutoff probability=45%	1 (1)	3 (8)	12 (24)	6 (17)	0 (0)	11 (21)
Cutoff probability=60%	0 (0)	0 (0)	0 (0)	0 (0)	0 (0)	0 (0)
Current Account						
Cutoff probability=45%	0 (0)	4 (4)	6 (24)	21 (23)	0 (0)	13 (24)
Cutoff probability=60%	0 (0)	4 (4)	6 (24)	21 (23)	0 (0)	13 (24)
Capital Account						
Cutoff probability=45%	4 (24)	0 (0)	2 (2)	0 (0)	0 (0)	2 (2)
Cutoff probability=60%	4 (24)	0 (0)	2 (2)	0 (0)	0 (0)	2 (2)
Financial Sector						
Cutoff probability=45%	2 (2)	0 (0)	10 (23)	0 (0)	0 (0)	1 (7)
Cutoff probability=60%	0 (0)	0 (0)	0 (0)	0 (0)	0 (0)	0 (0)
Real Sector						
Cutoff probability=45%	0 (0)	0 (0)	0 (0)	0 (0)	0 (0)	0 (0)
Cutoff probability=60%	0 (0)	0 (0)	0 (0)	0 (0)	0 (0)	0 (0)
Fiscal Sector						
Cutoff probability=45%	0 (0)	0 (0)	0 (0)	0 (0)	0 (0)	0 (0)
Cutoff probability=60%	0 (0)	0 (0)	0 (0)	0 (0)	0 (0)	0 (0)
Global Economy						
Cutoff probability=45%	0 (0)	0 (0)	0 (0)	0 (0)	0 (0)	0 (0)
Cutoff probability=60%	0 (0)	0 (0)	0 (0)	0 (0)	0 (0)	0 (0)

Note: Figures without parentheses refer to the number of signals, while those in parentheses refer to the lead time of the first signal.
Source: Author's estimates.

of signaling indicators increases from 3 in December 1996 to 8 in November 1997 for Indonesia, from 2 in early 1996 to 9 in mid-1997 for Korea, from 4–5 in late 1996 to 14 in July 1997 for Malaysia, from 3 in mid-1995 to 8 in early 1997 for the Philippines, and from 4 in early 1996 to 8–9 in mid-1997 for Thailand.

Table 4.18 shows the number of warning signals issued by each of the 40 selected leading indicators during the 24 months prior to the 1997 currency crisis for each of the six countries. For Indonesia, 11 leading indicators issue a total of 95 warning signals, including 7 by current account indicators, 37 by capital account indicators, 41 by financial sector indicators, 4 by real sector indicators, and 6 by global economy indicators. Two of the five top indicators issue warning signals—6 by the ratio of short-term external debt to foreign reserves and 10 by the ratio of M2 to foreign reserves.

For Korea, 11 leading indicators issue a total of 112 warning signals, including 12 by current account indicators, 22 by capital account indicators, 37 by financial sector indicators, 11 by real sector indicators, 24 by fiscal sector indicators, and 6 by global indicators. One top indicator, the real exchange rate, issues 4 signals.

For Malaysia, 19 leading indicators issue a total of 177 warning signals, including 20 by current account indicators, 71 by capital account indicators, 78 by financial sector indicators, and 8 by global indicators. Three of the five top indicators issue a total of 9 signals.

For the Philippines, 13 leading indicators issue a total of 155 warning signals, including 47 by current account indicators, 12 by capital account indicators, 43 by financial sector indicators, 2 by real sector indicators, 43 by fiscal sector indicators, and 8 by global indicators. One top indicator, the real exchange rate, issues 21 signals.

For Singapore, 8 leading indicators issue a total of 64 warning signals, including 16 by current account indicators, 31 by capital account indicators, 6 by financial sector indicators, 3 by real sector indicators, and 8 by global economy indicators. None of the top indicators issues warning signals.

And finally, for Thailand, 16 leading indicators issue a total of 167 warning signals, including 31 by current account indicators, 56 by capital account indicators, 59 by financial sector indicators, 13 by real sector indicators, and 8 by global indicators. One top indicator issues 13 warning signals.

Across the six countries, then, the number of warning signals is highest for Malaysia, followed by Thailand, Philippines, Korea, Indonesia, and Singapore. The number of warning signals from the top five indicators is highest for Thailand, followed by the Philippines; then Indonesia, Malaysia, and Korea; and finally Singapore.

Figures 4.7–4.12 **Number of Signaling Indicators in the Currency Crisis Model, 1970–1997**
Specific dates indicate crisis episodes

4.7 **Indonesia**

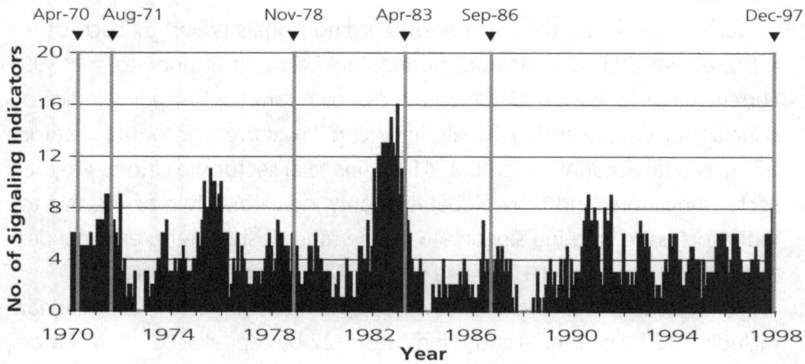

4.8 **Korea**

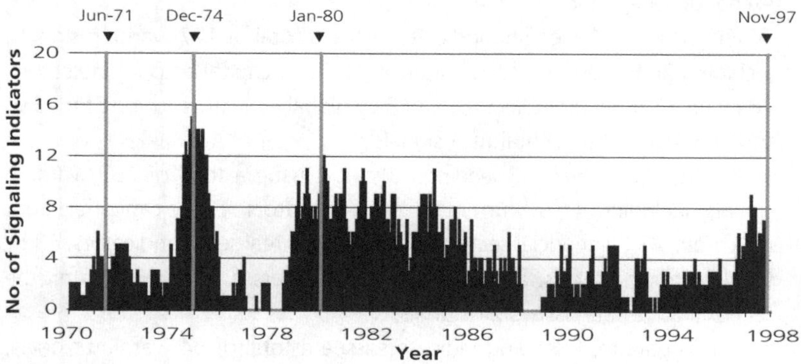

4.9 **Malaysia**

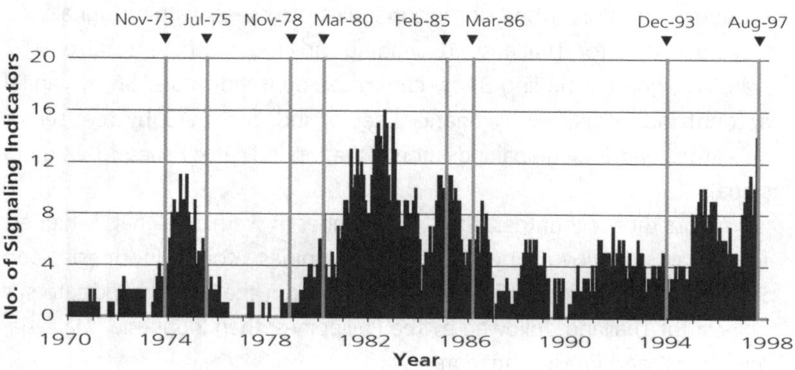

4.10 **Philippines**

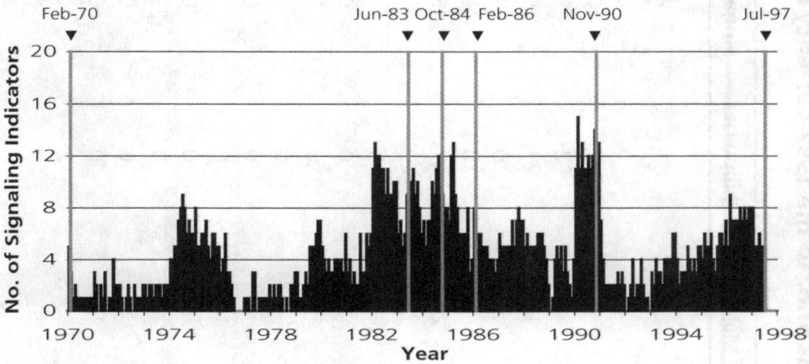

4.11 **Singapore**

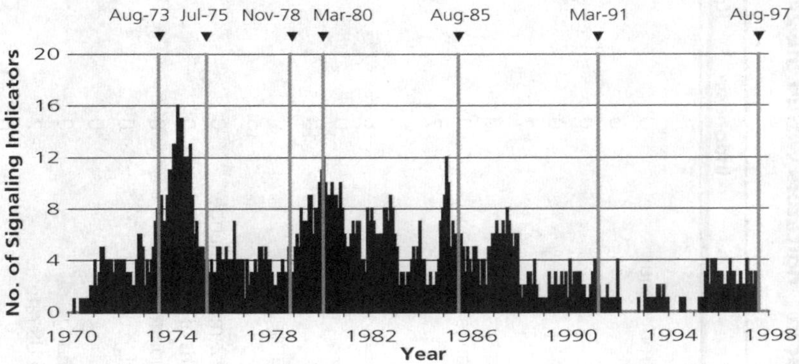

4.12 **Thailand**

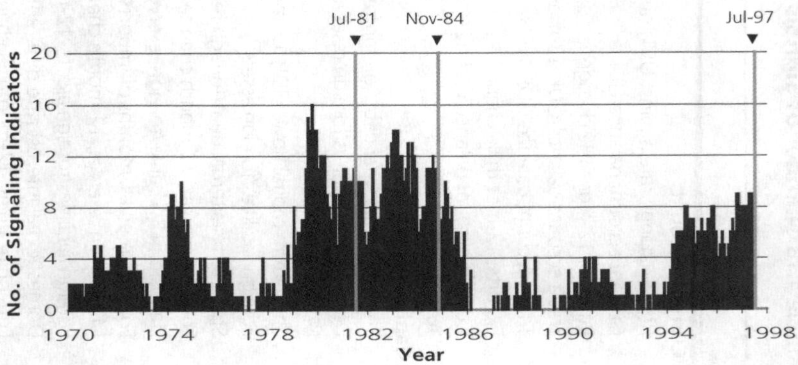

Table 4.18 **Number of Signals by Leading Indicators within the 24 Months prior to the 1997 Currency Crisis**

	Indonesia	Korea	Malaysia	Philippines	Singapore	Thailand
Current Account						
Real exchange rate against US$, deviation from trend	0	4	6	21	0	13
Current account balance/GDI	0	0	0	0	0	0
Imports, 12-month % change	0	0	0	1	0	0
Trade account balance/GDP, 12-month change	0	1	2	2	0	1
Trade account balance/GDP	7	0	12	23	0	11
Exports, 12-month % change	0	7	0	0	4	6
Current account balance/GDI, 12-month change	0	0	0	0	12	0
Total	**7**	**12**	**20**	**47**	**16**	**31**
Capital Account						
Short-term external debt/foreign reserves	6	0	2	0	0	0
Deposits in BIS banks/foreign reserves	0	0	0	0	0	0
M2/foreign reserves	10	0	1	0	0	0
Short-term capital flows/GDP, 12-month change	0	0	0	0	0	13
Foreign liabilities/foreign assets	19	0	8	0	0	24
Short-term external debt/foreign reserves, 12-month change	0	0	14	0	3	0
Foreign reserves, 12-month change in months of imports	0	0	5	0	0	0
Deposits in BIS banks/foreign reserves, 12-month change	0	8	6	0	23	0
Foreign reserves, months of imports covered	0	0	9	0	0	0
M2/foreign reserves, 12-month change	0	0	12	0	0	2
Foreign liabilities/foreign assets, 12-month change	0	0	5	12	0	13
Domestic real interest rate differential from US rate	2	9	0	0	0	0
Foreign reserves, 12-month % change	0	5	9	0	5	4
Total	**37**	**22**	**71**	**12**	**31**	**56**

Financial Sector						
Real commercial bank deposits, 12-month % change	0	0	0	0	0	0
Lending-deposit rate spread	0	0	0	1	0	0
Lending-deposit rate spread, 12-month change	0	0	0	0	0	1
Deposits/M2, 12-month change	0	0	7	0	0	4
Deposits/M2	0	24	0	0	0	0
Real interest rate	4	0	0	0	0	0
Loans/deposits, 12-month change	1	0	15	12	6	6
Loans/deposits	0	0	8	0	0	24
M1/GDP	12	0	24	6	0	0
Domestic credit/GDP	24	13	24	24	0	24
Total	**41**	**37**	**78**	**43**	**6**	**59**
Real Sector						
CPI, 12-month % change	0	0	0	0	0	0
Stock prices in US$, 12-month % change	4	11	0	2	3	13
Total	**4**	**11**	**0**	**2**	**3**	**13**
Fiscal Sector						
Central bank credit to public sector/GDP	0	0	0	19	0	0
Government consumption/GDP	0	24	0	24	0	0
Fiscal balance/GDP	0	0	0	0	0	0
Total	**0**	**24**	**0**	**43**	**0**	**0**
Global Economy						
Oil price in US$, 12-month % change	0	0	0	0	0	0
Real US$/yen exchange rate, deviation from trend	6	6	8	8	8	8
US real interest rate	0	0	0	0	0	0
US annual growth	0	0	0	0	0	0
Total	**6**	**6**	**8**	**8**	**8**	**8**

BIS = Bank for International Settlements, CPI = consumer price index, GDI = gross domestic investment, GDP = gross domestic product, M1 = narrow money, M2 = broad money.

Source: Author's estimates.

The Banking Crisis EWS Model

CRISIS PROBABILITIES

Figures 4.13–4.18 plot the time series of crisis probabilities monthly from 1970 to 1997, estimated on the basis of Composite I. As noted, crisis probabilities before 1996 are in-sample estimates while those for 1996 and 1997 are out-of-sample predictions. The specified dates indicate the start of banking crises.

The figures show that the banking crisis EWS model is less successful in predicting banking crises. Although the model reveals signs of increased banking sector vulnerability among the five countries suffering a banking crisis in 1997, only in Malaysia and Thailand does the crisis probability reach the 30% level. In the other three countries, the crisis probability remains below 20% in the run-up to the crisis. These results are far less satisfactory compared with the currency crisis EWS model. As pointed out by GKR, the weaker performance of the banking crisis EWS model compared with the currency crisis model may reflect the difficulty in accurately identifying starting dates for banking crises. More work is certainly required in this area. However, considering that the unconditional crisis probability is only 10% for banking crises in the sample, and our banking crisis EWS model manages to produce a crisis probability of over 30% for Malaysia and Thailand prior to the 1997 crisis, the model's performance could still be considered impressive.

To see whether sector-specific composite indexes perform any better than the general composite indexes in predicting the 1997 banking crisis, Figures 4.19–4.24 plot monthly time series of crisis probabilities estimated from the financial sector composite index, the best performer of the six. We find that in the case of the banking crisis model, the best sector composite index indeed outperforms the better general composite index in predicting the 1997 crisis. In all five sample countries seriously affected by the 1997 crisis, there are significant increases in the crisis probability during the 24 months prior to the crisis episode, reaching about 40% for many months. In four of the crisis-affected countries (the exception being Malaysia), the crisis probability rises to as high as 56% for certain months.

WARNING SIGNALS BY COMPOSITE INDEXES AND LEAD TIME

Table 4.19 reports the number of warning signals issued by various composite indexes and their lead time at the two cutoff probability levels, 30% and 50%. The two general composite indexes issue warning signals only at the 30% cutoff probability. Composite I issues 4 signals for Malaysia and 8 signals for Thailand, both with a lead time of 8 months. Composite II issues 1 signal for Thailand with a lead time of 3 months. There are no warning signals from the two composite indexes for the other countries. Among the sector composite indexes, only the financial sector index flashes. At the 30% cutoff probability, the financial sector composite index issues signals for all five countries where a banking crisis occurred: 1 for Indonesia, 6 for Korea, 9 for Malaysia, 18 for the Philippines, and 14 for Thailand. At the 50% cutoff level, it issues signals for four crisis-affected countries: 1 each for Indonesia and Korea with a lead time of 5–6 months, 4 for the Philippines with a lead time of 18 months, and 8 for Thailand with a lead time of 24 months. No signals are issued by any of the other sector composite indexes.

WARNING SIGNALS BY INDIVIDUAL LEADING INDICATORS

Figures 4.25–4.30 plot the number of leading indicators signaling in each month during the entire 1970–1997 period. As we can see, in most cases, the number of signaling indicators tends to increase when a crisis approaches. Prior to the 1997 crisis, the number of signaling indicators increases from 5–6 in 1996 to 7–8 in 1997 for Indonesia, from 2 in early 1996 to 9–11 in early 1997 for Korea, from 2–4 in the first half of 1996 to 8–12 in 1997 for Malaysia, from 4–6 in early 1994 to 9–11 in 1997 for the Philippines, and from 4–7 in the first half of 1996 to 13–14 in the first half of 1997 for Thailand.

We also count the number of signals issued by individual indicators during the 24 months prior to the 1997 crisis, as reported in Table 4.20.

For Indonesia, 16 leading indicators issue a total of 119 signals, including 38 by capital account indicators, 63 by financial sector indicators, 12 by real sector indicators, and 6 by global indicators. Three of the five top indicators issue signals—24 by the ratio of foreign liabilities to foreign assets, 9 by 12-month change in the real domestic interest rate, and 18 by the ratio of short-term external debt to foreign reserves.

For Korea, 11 indicators issue a total of 139 signals, including 12 by current account indicators, 16 by capital account indicators, 69 by financial sector indicators, 14 by real sector indicators, 22 by fiscal sector indicators, and 6 by global indicators. None of the top five indicators issues signals.

For Malaysia, 16 indicators issue a total of 129 signals, including 4 by current account indicators, 40 by capital account indicators, 73 by financial sector indicators, 4 by fiscal sector indicators, and 8 by global economy indicators. Among the five top indicators, three issue signals—11 by the ratio of foreign liabilities to foreign assets of the banking sector, 4 by months of imports covered by foreign reserves, and 8 by the ratio of short-term external debt to foreign reserves.

For the Philippines, 15 indicators issue a total of 186 signals, including 1 by current account indicators, 28 by capital account indicators, 94 by financial

Figures 4.13–4.18 **Banking Crises and Crisis Probabilities Predicted by Composite I, 1970–1997**
Specific dates indicate crisis episodes

4.13 **Indonesia**

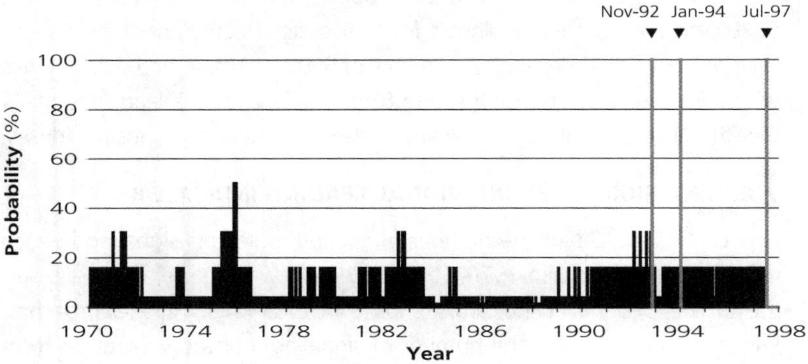

4.14 **Korea**

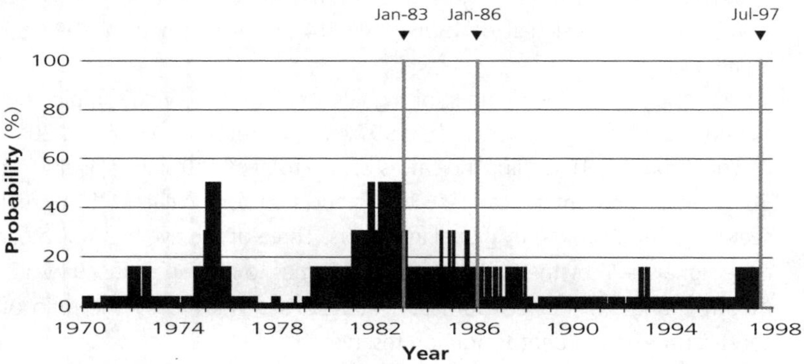

4.15 **Malaysia**

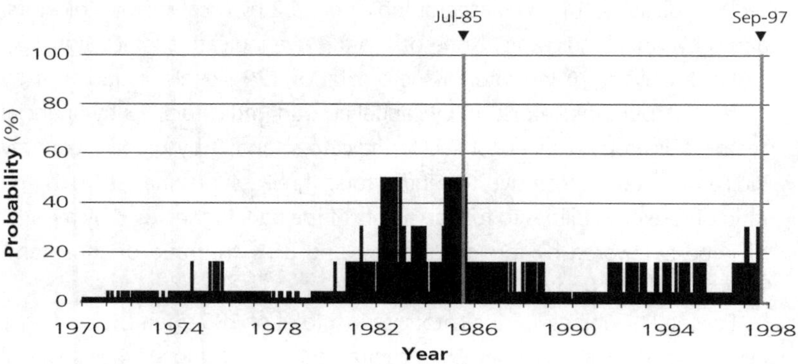

4.16 **Philippines**

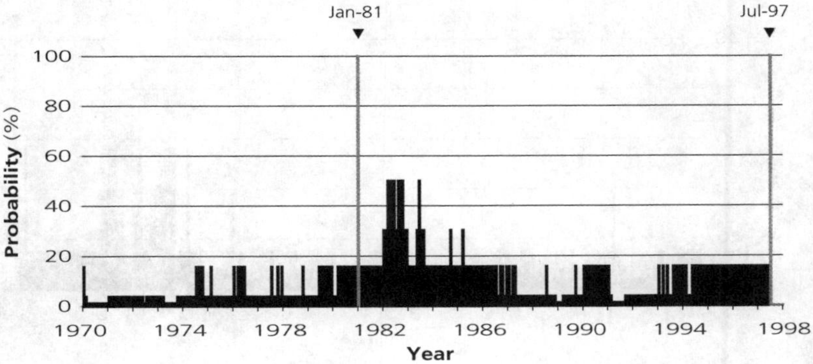

4.17 **Singapore**

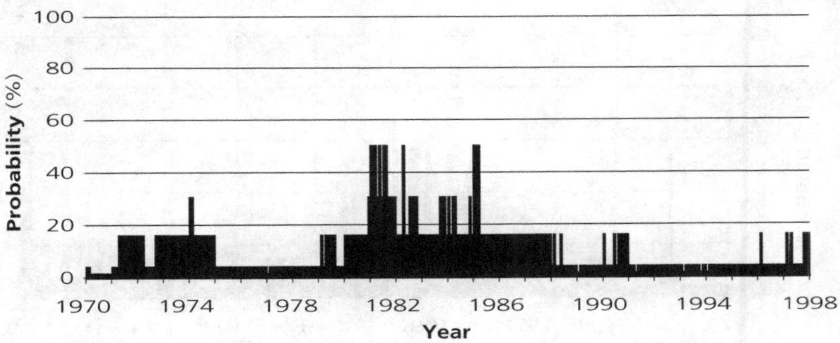

4.18 **Thailand**

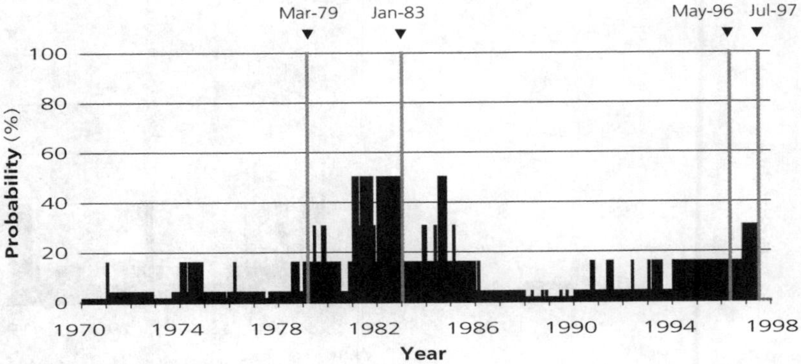

Figures 4.19–4.24 **Banking Crises and Crisis Probabilities Predicted by the Financial Sector Composite Index, 1970–1997**
Specific dates indicate crisis episodes

4.19 **Indonesia**

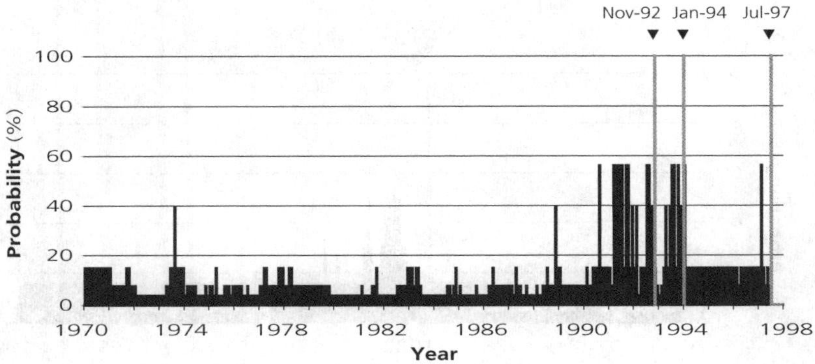

4.20 **Korea**

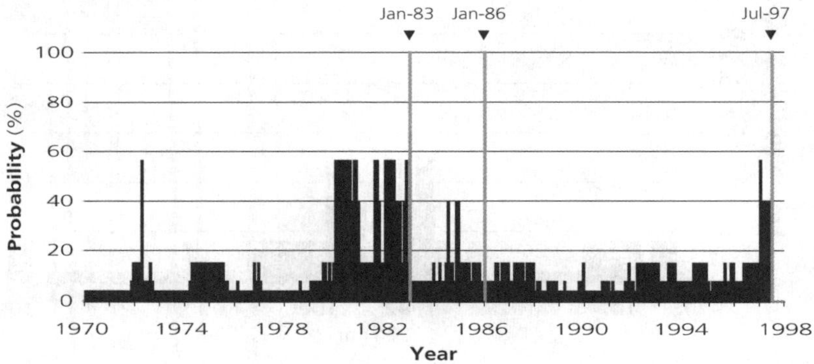

4.21 **Malaysia**

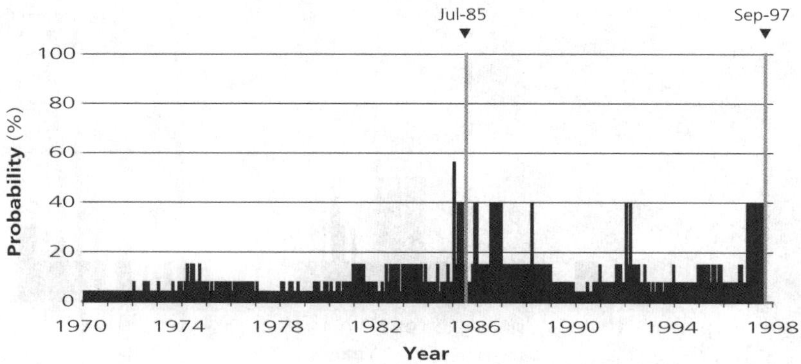

4.22 **Philippines**

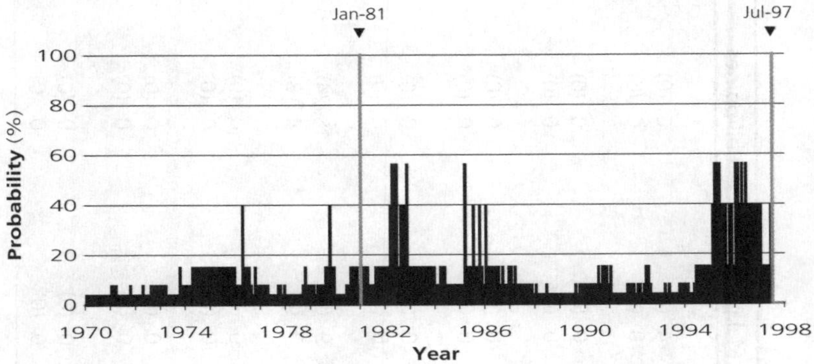

4.23 **Singapore**

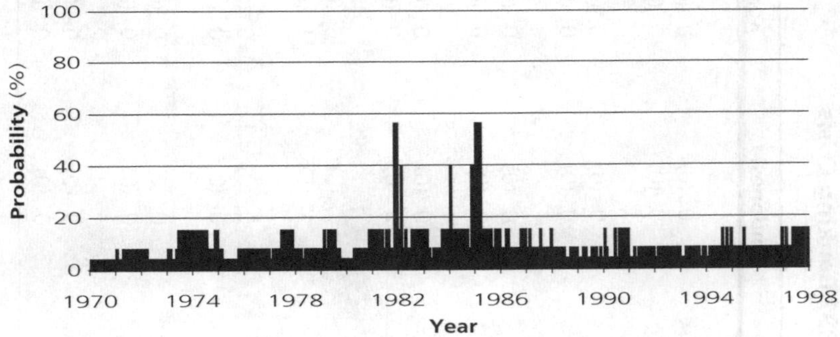

4.24 **Thailand**

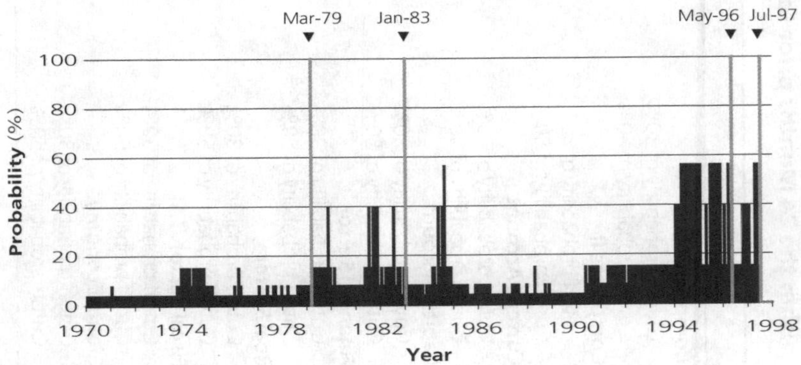

Table 4.19 **Number of Signals and Lead Time (in months) of Composite Indexes within the 24 Months prior to the 1997 Banking Crisis**

	Indonesia	Korea	Malaysia	Philippines	Thailand
Composite I					
Cutoff probability of 30%	0 (0)	0 (0)	4 (8)	0 (0)	8 (8)
Cutoff probability of 50%	0 (0)	0 (0)	0 (0)	0 (0)	0 (0)
Composite II					
Cutoff probability of 30%	0 (0)	0 (0)	0 (0)	0 (0)	1 (3)
Cutoff probability of 50%	0 (0)	0 (0)	0 (0)	0 (0)	0 (0)
Current Account					
Cutoff probability of 30%	0 (0)	0 (0)	0 (0)	0 (0)	0 (0)
Cutoff probability of 50%	0 (0)	0 (0)	0 (0)	0 (0)	0 (0)
Capital Account					
Cutoff probability of 30%	0 (0)	0 (0)	0 (0)	0 (0)	0 (0)
Cutoff probability of 50%	0 (0)	0 (0)	0 (0)	0 (0)	0 (0)
Financial Sector					
Cutoff probability of 30%	1 (5)	6 (6)	9 (9)	18 (24)	14 (24)
Cutoff probability of 50%	1 (5)	1 (6)	0 (0)	4 (18)	8 (24)
Real Sector					
Cutoff probability of 30%	0 (0)	0 (0)	0 (0)	0 (0)	0 (0)
Cutoff probability of 50%	0 (0)	0 (0)	0 (0)	0 (0)	0 (0)
Fiscal Sector					
Cutoff probability of 30%	0 (0)	0 (0)	0 (0)	0 (0)	0 (0)
Cutoff probability of 50%	0 (0)	0 (0)	0 (0)	0 (0)	0 (0)
Global Economy					
Cutoff probability of 30%	0 (0)	0 (0)	0 (0)	0 (0)	0 (0)
Cutoff probability of 50%	0 (0)	0 (0)	0 (0)	0 (0)	0 (0)

Note: Figures without parentheses refer to the number of signals, while those in parentheses refer to the lead time of the first signal.
Source: Author's estimates.

sector indicators, 13 by real sector indicators, 42 by fiscal sector indicators, and 8 by global indicators. But none of the five top leading indicators issues signals.

Although Singapore did not experience a banking crisis in 1997, there are also warning signals. Ten indicators issue a total of 90 signals, including 8 by current account indicators, 38 by capital account indicators, 35 by financial sector indicators, 1 real sector indicator, and 8 by global indicators. But again, none of the top five issues signals.

Finally, for Thailand, 18 indicators issue 182 signals, including 11 by current account indicators, 35 by capital account indicators, 104 by financial sector indicators, 24 by real sector indicators, and 8 by global indicators. Two of the top five indicators issue signals—24 by the ratio of foreign liabilities to foreign assets of the banking sector and 1 by the ratio of short-term external debt to foreign reserves.

Across the six countries, the total number of warning signals is the highest for the Philippines, followed by Thailand, Korea, Malaysia, Indonesia, and Singapore. The number of warning signals issued by the top five indicators is highest for Indonesia and Thailand, followed by Malaysia.

Figures 4.25–4.30 **Number of Signaling Indicators in the Banking Crisis Model, 1970–1997**
Specific dates indicate crisis episodes

4.25 **Indonesia**

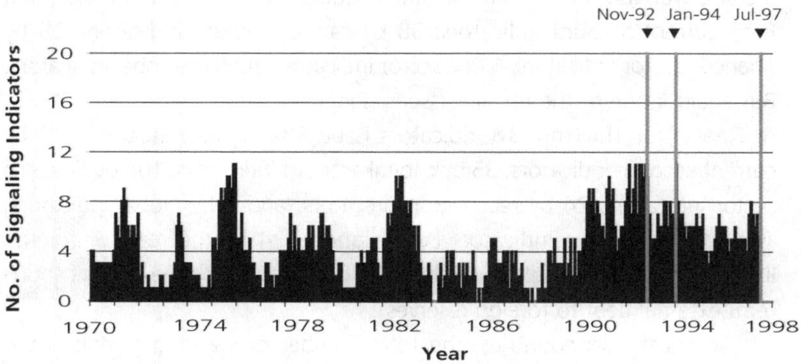

4.26 **Korea**

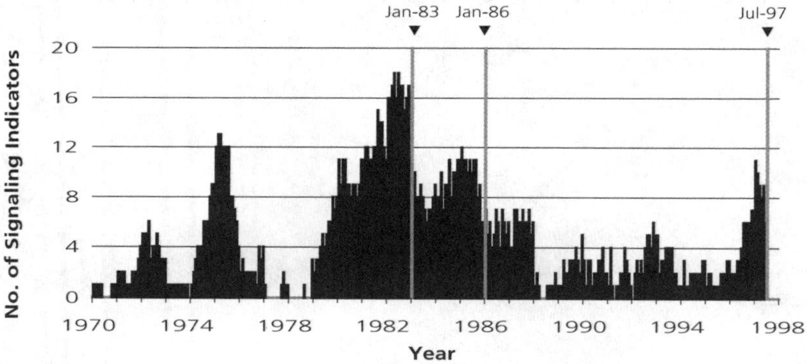

4.27 **Malaysia**

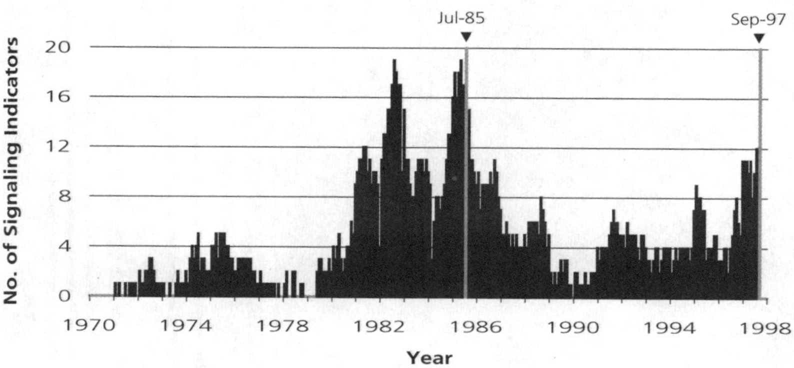

4.28 **Philippines**

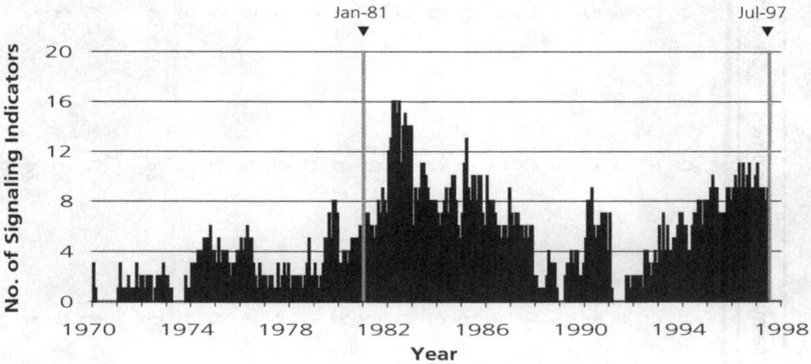

4.29 **Singapore**

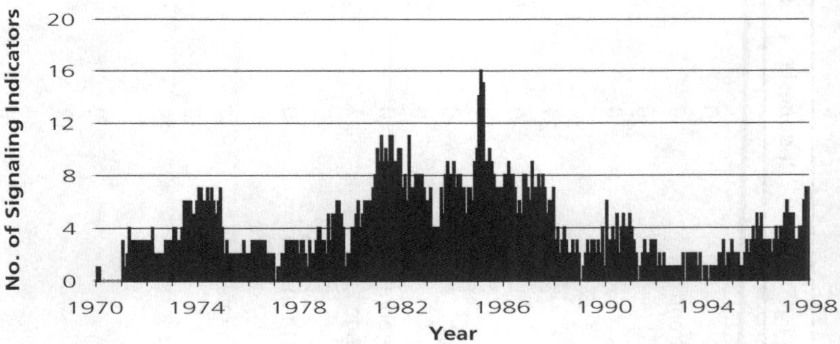

4.30 **Thailand**

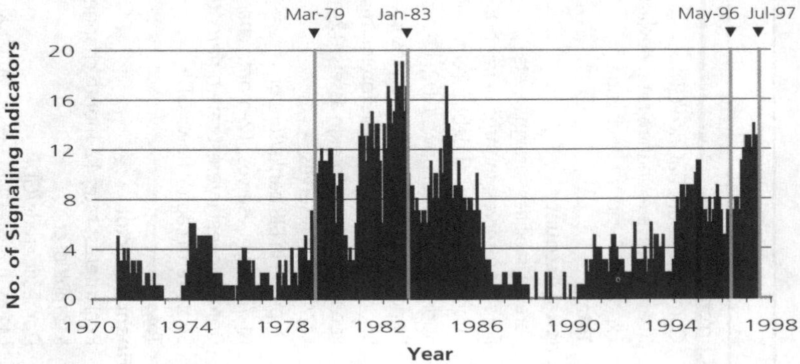

Table 4.20 **Number of Signals by Leading Indicators within the 24 Months prior to the 1997 Banking Crisis**

	Indonesia	Korea	Malaysia	Philippines	Singapore	Thailand
Current Account						
Current account balance/GDI	0	0	0	0	0	0
Real effective exchange rate, deviation from trend	0	0	0	1	0	0
Exports, 12-month % change	0	12	4	0	8	11
Total	**0**	**12**	**4**	**1**	**8**	**11**
Capital Account						
Foreign liabilities/foreign assets	24	0	11	0	0	24
Foreign reserves, months of imports covered	0	0	4	0	0	0
Short-term external debt/foreign reserves	18	0	8	0	0	1
Short term capital flows/GDP, 12-month change	0	0	0	0	0	13
Deposits in BIS banks/foreign reserves	0	0	0	0	0	0
Short-term external debt/foreign reserves, 12-month change	0	0	8	0	0	0
Foreign liabilities/foreign assets, 12-month change	6	0	8	16	3	13
M2/foreign reserves	10	0	1	0	0	0
Deposits in BIS banks/foreign reserves, 12-month change	0	0	6	0	17	0
M2/foreign reserves, 12-month change	0	0	9	0	0	1
Domestic real interest rate differential from US rate	4	16	0	0	0	0
Short-term capital flows/GDP	0	0	0	12	18	7
Total	**38**	**16**	**40**	**28**	**38**	**35**
Financial Sector						
Real interest rate, 12-month change	9	0	0	0	0	0
M2 multiplier	19	24	0	23	24	17
Domestic credit/GDP	24	18	24	24	4	24
M2 multiplier, 12-month % change	2	16	0	8	1	0
Domestic credit/GDP, 12-month change	3	10	17	24	0	16

Real interest rate	4	0	0	0	0	0
Lending-deposit rate spread, 12-month change	0	0	0	0	0	1
Loans/deposits, 12-month change	1	0	15	12	6	6
Lending-deposit rate spread	0	1	0	3	0	0
Loans/deposits	0	0	8	0	0	24
Real commercial bank deposits, 12-month % change	1	0	0	0	0	10
Deposits/M2, 12-month change	0	0	9	0	0	6
Total	**63**	**69**	**73**	**94**	**35**	**104**
Real Sector						
Stock prices in local currency, 12-month % change	1	11	0	6	1	13
Industrial production index, 12-month % change	11	3	0	7	0	11
Total	**12**	**14**	**0**	**13**	**1**	**24**
Fiscal Sector						
Net credit to public sector/GDP	0	0	0	24	0	0
Central bank credit to public sector/GDP	0	0	0	18	0	0
Central bank credit to public sector/GDP, 12-month change	0	0	4	0	0	0
Government consumption/GDP	0	22	0	24	0	0
Fiscal balance/GDP	0	0	0	0	0	0
Net credit to public sector/GDP, 12-month change	0	0	0	0	0	0
Total	**0**	**22**	**4**	**42**	**0**	**0**
Global Economy						
US real interest rate	0	0	0	0	0	0
Oil price in US$	0	0	0	0	0	0
US real interest rate, 12-month change	0	0	0	0	0	0
US annual growth	0	0	0	0	0	0
Real US$/yen exchange rate, deviation from trend	6	6	8	8	8	8
Total	**6**	**6**	**8**	**8**	**8**	**8**

BIS = Bank for International Settlements, GDI = gross domestic investment, GDP = gross domestic product, M2 = broad money.
Source: Author's estimates.

4.6 Summary and Conclusions

In this chapter, we have described two nonparametric EWS models, one for currency crises and the other for banking crises, estimated using the data of six East Asian countries for 1970–1995. We then applied the models to data for 1996 and 1997 to predict the 1997 financial crises as out-of-sample tests.

The Currency Crisis EWS Model

Defining a currency crisis as an episode of monthly depreciation of a domestic currency against the US dollar exceeding the sample mean by two standard deviations, the currency crisis model identified 28 currency crisis episodes in the six countries during the sample period, and selected 40 leading indicators out of more than 60 economic and financial indicators screened as predictors of these crisis episodes. Based on the 40 leading indicators, two general composite indexes (Composite I and Composite II) and six sector-specific composite indexes (current account, capital account, financial sector, real sector, fiscal sector, and global economy) were constructed.

Among the 40 selected leading indicators, 9 have an *NSR* smaller than 0.5, meaning that the probability of their issuing true warning signals is at least twice as high as the probability of issuing false signals:

- deviation of the real exchange rate against the US dollar from its trend,
- ratio of short-term external debt to foreign reserves,
- ratio of deposits in BIS banks to foreign reserves,
- ratio of M2 to foreign reserves,
- 12-month change in the ratio of short-term capital flows to GDP,
- ratio of foreign liabilities to foreign assets of the banking sector,
- 12-month change in the ratio of short-term external debt to foreign reserves,
- ratio of current account balance to GDI, and
- 12-month percentage change in real commercial bank deposits.

Seven of these 9 indicators have a conditional crisis probability of 50% or above, meaning that when any one of them issues a warning signal, there is at least a 50% chance that a currency crisis will follow within 24 months.

Results of in-sample evaluation show that composite indexes predict most of the currency crisis episodes during 1970–1995 in the six sample countries. The weighted general composite index (Composite I) issues early warning signals prior to 18 of the 24 crisis episodes included in the in-sample evaluation at a cutoff probability of 60%. The unweighted general composite index (Composite II) flashes prior to 18 crisis episodes, but at a lower cutoff probability of 45%. Among the sector composite indexes, the current account and capital account indexes outperform others, with each predicting 14–15 crisis episodes at a cutoff probability of 60%. Performance of other sector composite indexes is mixed.

The out-of-sample tests show that the weighted general composite index predicts the 1997 currency crisis in at least four of the five crisis-affected countries at the 60% cutoff probability, with early warning signals persistent and starting as early as 24 months prior to the crisis in Malaysia, Philippines, and Thailand. Among the six sector composite indexes, the current account index anticipates the 1997 crisis in all the crisis-affected countries with the exception of Indonesia, and the capital account index predicts the episodes in Indonesia, Malaysia, and Thailand, all at the 60% cutoff probability. The financial sector composite index predicts the crisis episodes in Indonesia, Malaysia, and Thailand at the cutoff probability of 45%. There are no warning signals from the other sector composite indexes prior to the 1997 crisis.

The Banking Crisis EWS Model

Using banking crisis episodes provided by GKR (where the beginning of a banking crisis was marked by bank runs; or closures, mergers, or takeovers of important financial institutions; or large-scale government assistance to the banking sector), the model identified 40 leading indicators out of more than 60 economic and financial indicators. Based on these, six sector and two general composite indexes were constructed.

Nineteen of the 40 selected leading indicators have an *NSR* smaller than 0.5. The top 10 leading indicators are

- ratio of foreign liabilities to foreign assets of the banking sector,
- months of imports covered by foreign reserves,
- US real interest rate,
- ratio of short-term external debt to foreign reserves,
- 12-month change in the domestic real interest rate,
- 12-month change in the ratio of short-term capital flows to GDP,
- ratio of deposits in BIS banks to foreign reserves,
- level of world oil prices in US dollars,

- ratio of net credit to the public sector to GDP, and
- 12-month change in the ratio of short-term external debt to foreign reserves.

Each of these top 10 indicators has an *NSR* ranging from 0.26 to 0.41, meaning that the probability of their issuing true signals is about three times as high as the probability of their issuing false signals, and each has a conditional crisis probability ranging from 22% to 36%.

Results of in-sample evaluation show that the weighted general composite index, Composite I, predicts 6 of the 8 identified banking crisis episodes at the cutoff probability of 30%, and 3 at the cutoff probability of 50%. Among the sector composite indexes, the financial sector composite index predicts 7 banking crisis episodes at the cutoff probability of 30%, and 4 at the 50% cutoff level. The fiscal sector composite index predicts 2 episodes at the 30% cutoff probability and 1 at the 50% cutoff level. None of the banking crisis episodes during 1970–1995 is predicted by the other sector composite indexes.

The out-of-sample tests show that the 1997 banking crises in Malaysia and Thailand are predicted by Composite I at the cutoff probability of 30%, with a lead time of as early as 8 months. The financial sector composite index predicts the crisis episodes in at least four of the five crisis-affected countries at the cutoff probability of 30%, with warning signals persistent and starting as early as 24 months prior to the episodes in the Philippines and Thailand. At the cutoff probability of 50%, it still predicts the crisis in Indonesia, Korea, Philippines, and Thailand, although with fewer warning signals and a shorter lead time. There are no warning signals from the other sector composite indexes.

In sum, this chapter shows that the two EWS models have reasonably good predictive power, especially when compared with most EWS models reported in other studies. Between the two models, the currency crisis EWS performs better than the banking crisis EWS. Overall, the weighted general composite index (Composite I) appears most reliable. But three sector-specific composite indexes also have significant predictive power: the current account and capital account indexes for the currency crisis model, and the financial sector index for the banking crisis model.

Areas for Further Work

Despite these encouraging findings, there remain many areas where further research is needed to improve the performance of the two EWS models, and EWS modeling in general. At their current state of development, EWS models can be useful tools in assisting policy analysis and policy making, but their limitations have to be fully understood and appreciated. The following areas are of particular importance for further research.

DATING CRISES

In dating currency crises, this study did not make a distinction in the severity of the currency depreciation episodes. Those "true crises" that had far-reaching systemic economic impact were not distinguished from the more benign episodes (some of which may not even have been considered "crises" at the time they occurred). Distinguishing between these two types of currency depreciations is likely to improve the performance of the currency crisis models. In the case of banking crises, further work is required to determine their starting dates more accurately.

ADDITIONAL INDICATORS

The range of leading indicators used in the EWS models remains limited. In particular, given data constraints, this study did not use many prudential indicators measuring balance sheet soundness, asset quality, and profitability of banks. Indicators directly capturing regional contagion effects need to be examined. And indicators of political stability could also be explored.

DATA TRANSFORMATION

There remain many questions about the appropriate form or forms each indicator should take in an EWS model. Data transformation for the real exchange rate is a particularly important issue. The common practice of using a deterministic time trend as a proxy for the long run equilibrium real exchange rate, assuming it to be linear, log-linear or exponential, is theoretically difficult to justify and practically problematic. This study used the theoretically more acceptable stochastic time trend estimated from a mathematical filter—the HP filter. But a stochastic trend also has its weakness, as highlighted earlier, and needs to be scrutinized more closely. A particular concern is that different methods of estimating trends can sometimes yield conflicting results as to whether there is an appreciation or depreciation of a real exchange rate. This concern becomes even more important if we consider that the real exchange rate is usually given a very large weight in constructing composite indexes in existing studies.

WEIGHTING SCHEMES OF COMPOSITE INDEXES

Many EWS models use weighted composite indexes with better performing indicators allotted larger weights. However, there can be objections to this and indeed any weighting scheme. One reason is that the weighted composite indexes are sensitive to any malfunction in better-performing leading indicators. For instance, we found that if the real exchange rate is excluded from the currency crisis model, its predictive performance weakens. Also, leading indicators and composite indexes that predict past crises well may not remain good at predicting future crises. Similarly, leading indicators and composite indexes that were not good at predicting past crises may become important in predicting future crises. Partly because of this problem, we proposed two general composite indexes and six sector composites. But for real time forecasting, we have to decide which should be adjudged most reliable, especially between the two general composite indexes. This requires further work.

REGIME SHIFTS

This is one reason why it has been difficult to predict future crises using past data. Over time, domestic economic structures and the international economic environment change. For example, the likelihood of contagion has increased as globalization has spread during the past decades. Similarly, the importance of the interaction between the financial system and foreign exchange regime has increased as access to foreign borrowing has grown along with the flow of short-term foreign capital. In addition, capital accounts have become more open in recent years in many countries, increasing the ease with which large capital outflows can take place. Deciding how far these shifts in institutional and policy regimes should be considered when developing EWS models is a big challenge.

FORECASTING TECHNIQUES

The forecasting technique commonly used in the signaling approach is not satisfactory. One shortcoming is that crisis probability of a particular month is estimated on the basis of data only for that month, and is thus independent of the probability estimates of previous months, that is, the system does not have a memory. Another shortcoming is that probability estimates do not make use of prior information on how frequent crises are in the sample, that is, the unconditional crisis probability. These two shortcomings could be addressed by using some statistical techniques such as the sequential probability model, widely used in estimating leading composite indicators of turning points in business cycles. This is another area for further work.

POLICY RESPONSES

So far, this study has focused only on constructing EWS models. We have not made any attempt to address the issue of policy responses. If an EWS model sends out warning signals, how should policymakers respond? This is obviously an important area for further work, but may be beyond the scope of this study.

References

Berg, Andrew, and Catherine Pattillo. 1999. Are Currency Crises Predictable: A Test. *IMF Staff Papers* 46 (2): 107–138.

Calvo, Guillermo. 1987. Balance of Payments Crises in a Cash-in-Advance Economy. *Journal of Money, Credit and Banking* 19 (February): 19–32.

Demirgüç-Kunt, Asli, and Enrica Detragiache. 1997. The Determinants of Banking Crises: Evidence from Developed and Developing Countries. *IMF Working Paper No. 97/106*. IMF, Washington DC, September.

———. 1998a. The Determinants of Banking Crises: Evidence from Developing and Developed Countries. *IMF Staff Papers* 45 (1): 81–109.

———. 1998b. Financial Liberalization and Financial Fragility. *IMF Working Paper No. 98/83*. IMF, Washington DC, March.

———. 1999. Monitoring Banking Sector Fragility: A Multivariate Logit Approach, *IMF Working Paper No. 99/147*. IMF, Washington DC, September.

Diaz-Alejandro, Carlo. 1985. Goodbye Financial Repression, Hello Financial Crash. *Journal of Development Economics* 19 (September–October): 1–24.

Edison, Hali J. 2000. Do Indicators of Financial Crises Work? An Evaluation of an Early Warning System. *International Finance Discussion Paper No. 675*. Board of Governors of the Federal Reserve System, Washington DC.

Eichengreen, Barry, Andrew K. Rose, and Charles Wyplosz. 1994. Speculative Attacks on Pegged Exchanged Rates: An Empirical Exploration with Special Reference to the Europe Monetary System. *NBER Working Papers* 4898: National Bureau of Economic Research (NBER), Cambridge.

Eichengreen, Barry, and Carlos Arteta. 2000. Banking Crises in Emerging Markets: Presumptions and Evidence. *Center for International and Development Economics Research Working Paper C00-115*. University of California, Berkeley.

Enders, Walter. 1995. *Applied Econometric Time-Series*. New York: John Wiley and Sons.

Frankel, Jeffrey A., and Andrew K. Rose. 1996. Exchange Rate Crises in Emerging Markets. *Journal of International Economics* 41 (3/4, November): 351–68.

Garber, Peter, Robin Lumsdaine, and Paolo Longato. 2001. *Deutsche Bank Alarm Clock: Descriptive Manual Version 3*. Global Markets Research, Deutsche Bank, London, October.

Goldstein, Morris, Graciella L. Kaminsky, and Carmen M. Reinhart. 2000. *Assessing Financial Vulnerability: An Early Warning System for Emerging Markets*. Washington DC: Institute for International Economics.

Hardy, Daniel, and Ceyla Pazarbasioglu. 1998. Leading Indicators of Banking Crises: Was Asia Different? *IMF Working Paper No. 98/91*. IMF, Washington DC, June.

Kaminsky, Graciela L., Saul Lizondo, and Carmen M. Reinhart. 1998. Leading Indicators of Currency Crises. *IMF Staff Papers* 45 No. 1 (March): 1–48.

Kaminsky, Graciela L. 1998. Currency and Banking Crises: Composite Leading Indicators. *International Finance Discussion Paper Series No. 629*. Board of Governors of the Federal Reserve System, Washington DC, October.

————. 1999. Currency and Banking Crises: The Early Warnings of Distress. *Working Paper*. George Washington University, Washington DC, February.

Kaminsky, Graciela L., and Carmen Reinhart. 1999. The Twin Crises: The Causes of Banking and Balance-of-Payments Problems. *American Economic Review* 89, No. 3 (June): 473–500.

————. 2002. Excessive Risk-Taking, Banking Sector Fragility, and Banking Crises. *Office of Research Working Paper No. 02–0114*. University of Illinois at Urbana-Champaign, Urbana-Champaign.

Kibritcioglu, Aykut. 1998. Financial Crises in Asia and Latin America: Then and Now. *American Economic Review* 88, No. 2 (May): 444–48.

Kim, S. H., M. A. Kose, and M. G. Plummer. 1999. Understanding the Asian Contagion: An International Business Cycle Perspective. *Manuscript No. 25*. International Centre for the Study of East Asian Development, Kitakyushu, December.

Krugman, P. 1979. A Model of Balance-of-Payments Crises. *Journal of Money, Credit, and Banking* (August): 311–25.

Lindgren, Carl-Johan, Gillian Garcia, and Matthew Saal. 1996. *Bank Soundness and Macroeconomic Policy*. Washington DC: International Monetary Fund.

Montiel, P., and C. M. Reinhart. 1997. The Dynamics of Capital Movements to Emerging Economies During the 1990s. Forthcoming in *Short-term Capital Movements and Balance of Payments Crises*, edited by S. Griffith-Jones and M. Montes. Helsinki: UNU/WIDER.

Obstfeld, Maurice. 1986. Rational and Self-Fulfilling Balance of Payments Crises. *American Economic Review* Vol. 76 (March): 72–81.

————. 1996. Models of Crises with Self-Fulfilling Features. *European Economic Review* Vol. 40 (April): 103–47.

Roy, Amlan. 2001. Emerging Markets Risk Indicator (EMRI). *Global Emerging Markets Strategy.* Credit Suisse First Boston, London, February.

Sachs, Jeffrey, Aaron Tornell, and Andrés Velasco. 1996. Financial Crises in Emerging Markets: The Lessons From 1995. *Brookings Papers on Economic Activity* 1: 147–215.

Sheng, Andrew. 1996. *Bank Restructuring: Lessons from the 1980s*. Washington DC: World Bank.

Sundararajan, V., Charles Enoch, Armida San José, Paul Hilbers, Russell Krueger, Marina Moretti, and Graham Slack. 2002. Financial Soundness Indicators:

Analytical Aspects and Country Practices. *IMF Occasional Paper No. 212*, IMF, Washington DC, April.

Velasco, Andrés. 1987. Financial Crises and Balance of Payments Crises: A Simple Model of the Southern Cone Experience. *Journal of Development Economics* Vol. 27 (October): 263–83.

Yoshitomi, Masaru, and Kenichi Ohno. 1999. Capital-Account Crisis and Credit Contraction: The New Nature of Crisis Requires New Policy Responses. *Working Paper No. 2,* ADB Institute, Tokyo, May.

APPENDIX 4.1

Currency Crisis Episodes and Predicted Crisis Probabilities—Alternative Models

Figures 4.A.1–4.A.6 **Currency Crises and Crisis Probabilities: Alternative Model I, 1970–1997** (based on a model using a linear trend for the real exchange rate)
Specific dates indicate crisis episodes

4.A.1 **Indonesia**

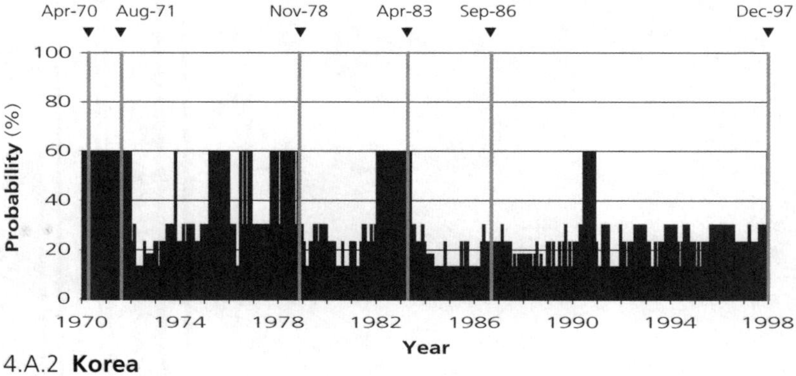

4.A.2 **Korea**

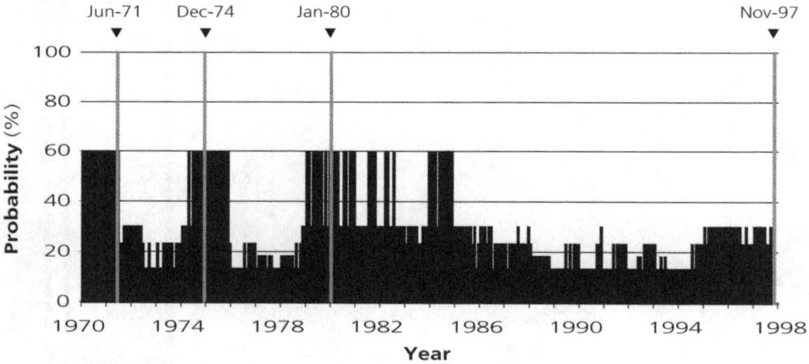

4.A.3 **Malaysia**

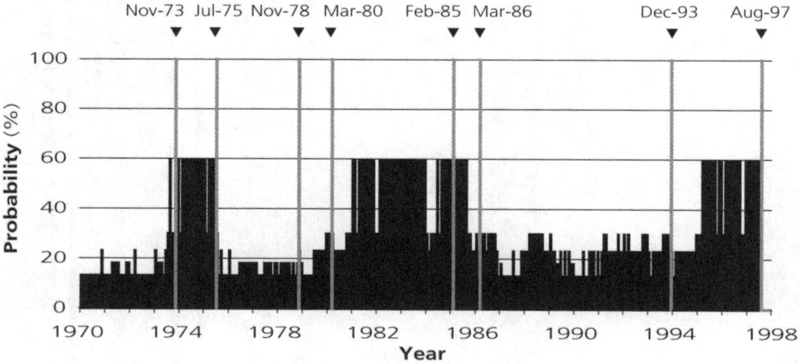

4.A.4 **Philippines**

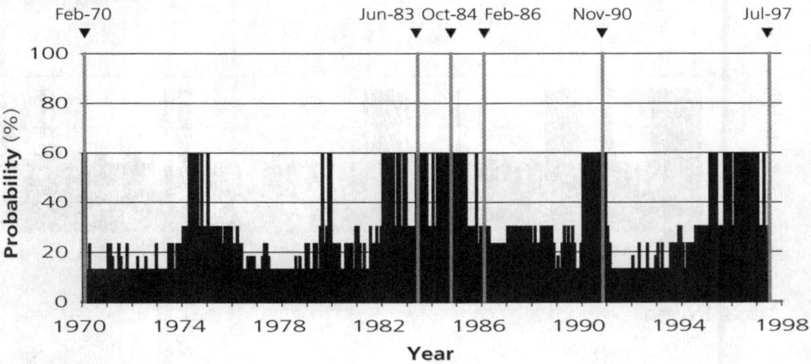

4.A.5 **Singapore**

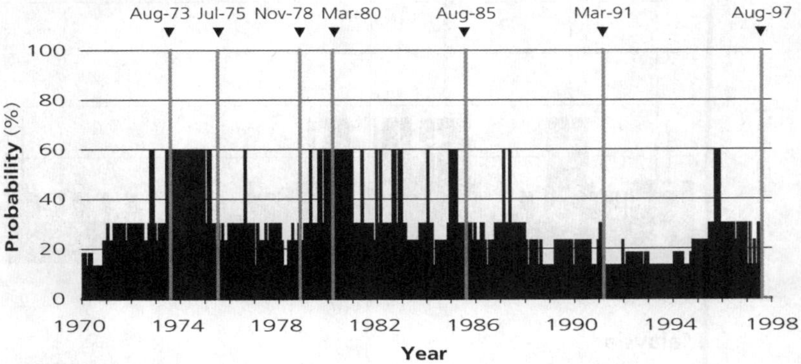

4.A.6 **Thailand**

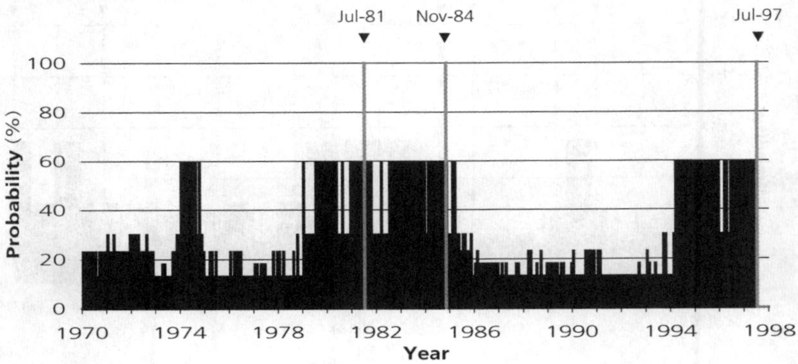

Figures 4.A.7–4.A.12 **Currency Crises and Crisis Probabilities: Alternative Model II, 1970–1997** (based on a model excluding the real exchange rate as a leading indicator)
Specific dates indicate crisis episodes

4.A.7 **Indonesia**

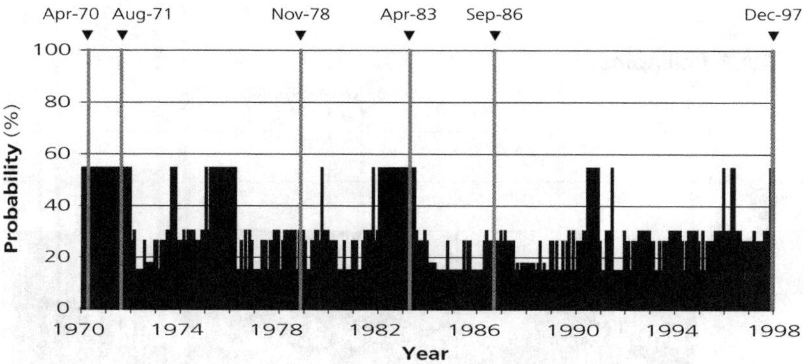

4.A.8 **Korea**

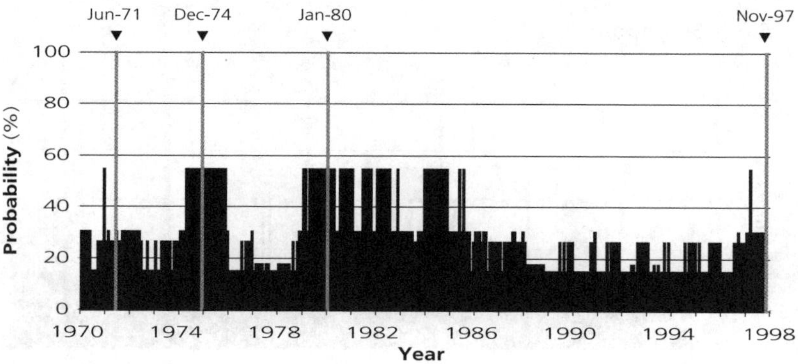

4.A.9 **Malaysia**

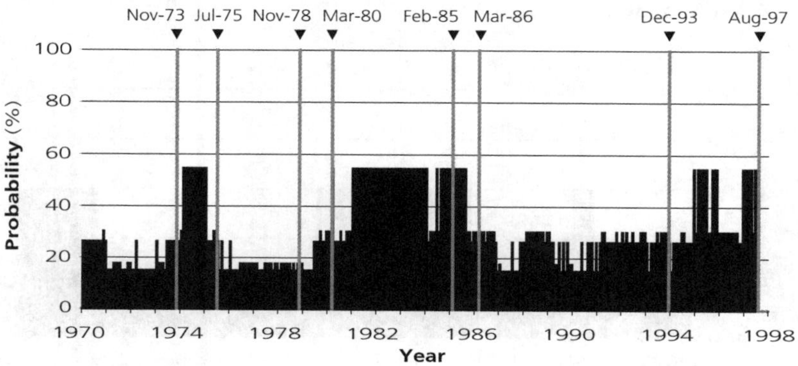

4.A.10 **Philippines**

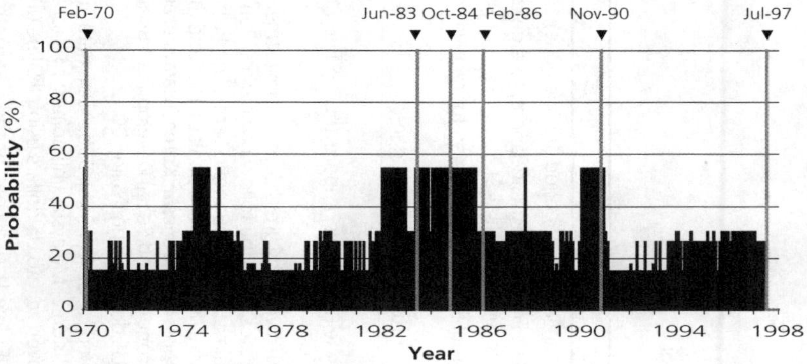

4.A.11 **Singapore**

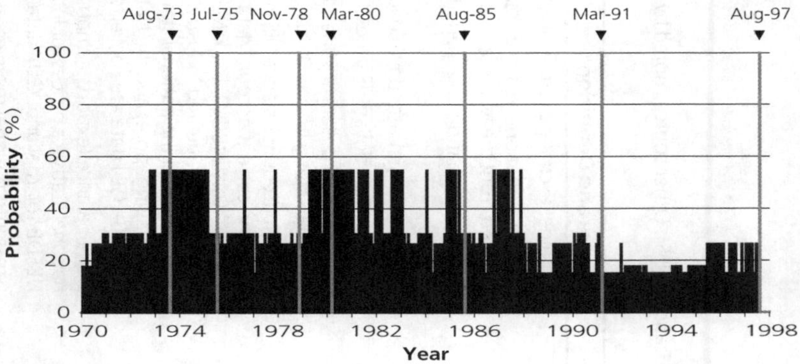

4.A.12 **Thailand**

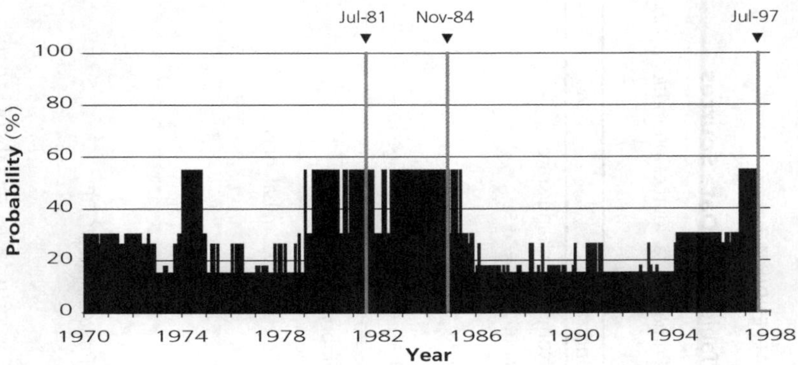

APPENDIX 4.2

Table 4.A.1 **Data Sources**

Primary Data Source: *International Financial Statistics* (IFS). Other sources noted by indicator.

Indicator	Source and Definition
Nominal exchange rate	Nominal exchange rate against the US dollar, end of period (IFS line 00ae).
Foreign reserves	Gross international reserves less gold (IFS line 1L.d). For Singapore, foreign exchange reserves sourced from the Monetary Authority of Singapore (MAS).
Real exchange rate	Nominal exchange rate, period average (IFS line 00rf) adjusted for relative consumer prices (IFS line 64).
Real effective exchange rate	JP Morgan estimates downloaded from http://www2.jpmorgan.com.
Exports	Exports in US dollars (IFS line 70d)
Imports	Imports in US dollars (IFS line 71d). For the Philippines, imports fob (IFS line 71v) converted into US dollars using IFS line 00rf.
Current account balance/GDI	Current account balance (IFS line 78ald) divided by gross domestic investment (IFS lines 93e plus 93l). The current account data are updated from the following sources: Bank Indonesia (BI); Bank of Korea (BOK); Bank Negara Malaysia (BNM); Bangko Sentral ng Pilipinas (BSP); the Ministry of Trade and Industry, Singapore (MTI); and the Bank of Thailand (BOT). GDI data are updated from the national statistics offices for Indonesia, Korea, Malaysia, and Philippines; the MTI for Singapore; and the National Economic and Social Development Board for Thailand (NESDB). GDI data are converted into US dollars using IFS line 00rf.
Trade balance/GDP	Trade balance (exports – imports) divided by GDP (IFS line 99b). GDP data are updated from the national statistics offices for Indonesia, Korea, Malaysia, Philippines; MTI for Singapore; and NESDB for Thailand. GDP data are converted into US dollars using IFS line 00rf.
Foreign reserves, months of imports	Gross international reserves less gold (IFS line 1L.d) divided by the 12-month moving average of monthly imports. For Singapore, foreign exchange reserves data are sourced from MAS.

M2/foreign reserves	M2 (IFS lines 34 plus 35) converted into US dollars using IFS line 00ae, divided by foreign reserves. For Korea, Philippines, and Thailand, M2 data are sourced from BOK, BSP, and BOT, respectively.
Short-term exernal debt/foreign reserves	External debt with maturity of less than 1 year divided by foreign reserves. External debt data are sourced from Bank for International Settlements (BIS) and Global Development Finance of the World Bank (GDF).
Short-term capital flow/GDP	Period on period change in external debt with maturity of less than 1 year (BIS and GDF) divided by GDP converted into US dollars using IFS line 00rf.
Deposits in BIS banks/foreign reserves	Deposits in BIS banks sourced from the Institute of International Finance divided by foreign reserves.
Domestic real interest rate differential from the US rate	Nominal interest rate (IFS line 60p) less inflation rate (line 64x) less US real interest rate (60P less 64x)
M2 multiplier	M2 (IFS lines 34 plus 35) divided by base money (IFS line 14). For Korea, Philippines, and Thailand, M2 data are sourced from BOK, BSP, and BOT, respectively.
Deposits/M2	Commercial bank deposits (IFS lines 24 plus 25) divided by M2. Commercial bank deposit data for Korea and Thailand are sourced from BOK and BOT, respectively.
Domestic credit/GDP	Domestic credit (IFS line 32) divided by GDP. For Thailand, domestic credit data are sourced from BOT.
M1/GDP	M1 (IFS line 34) divided by GDP.
Domestic real interest rate	Nominal interest rate (IFS line 60p) less inflation rate (IFS line 64x).
Lending-deposit rate spread	Lending rate (IFS line 60p) less deposit rate (IFS line 60l).
Real commercial bank deposits	Commercial bank deposits (IFS lines 24 plus 25) divided by consumer prices (IFS line 64). For Korea and Thailand, commercial bank deposit data are sourced from BOK and BOT, respectively.
Loans/deposits	Bank claims (IFS line 22a to 22d) divided by commercial bank deposits (IFS lines 24 plus 25). For Korea and Thailand, bank claims and commercial bank deposit data are sourced from BOK and BOT, respectively.
Inflation rate	12-month % change in the consumer price index (line 64).

Continued on next page

Table 4.A.1 (*Cont'd*)

Indicator	Source and Definition
Industrial production	Index of industrial production (IFS line 66c).
Equity prices	Stock price index (Bloomberg data).
US real interest rate	Nominal interest rate (IFS line 60p) less inflation rate (IFS line 64x).
US annual growth	GDP growth (US Bureau of Economic Analysis).
World oil price	Spot oil price (IFS line 00176aaz).
Real dollar/yen exchange rate	Nominal dollar/yen exchange rate (IFS line 00ae) adjusted for relative consumer prices (IFS line 64).
Fiscal deficit/GDP	Fiscal deficit (IFS line 80) divided by GDP. Fiscal deficit data are updated from the national statistics offices for Indonesia, Korea, Malaysia, Philippines; MTI for Singapore; and NESDB for Thailand.
Central bank credit to the public sector/GDP	Central bank credit to the public sector (IFS lines 12A to 12C) divided by GDP.
Net credit to the public sector/GDP	Claims on the public sector (IFS line 32A to 32C) divided by GDP.
Government consumption/GDP	Government consumption (IFS line 91f) divided by GDP (IFS line 99b). Government consumption data are updated from the national statistics offices for Indonesia, Korea, Malaysia, Philippines; MTI for Singapore; and NESDB for Thailand.

BIS = Bank for International Settlements, GDI = gross domestic investment, GDP = gross domestic product, M1 = narrow money, M2 = broad money.

CHAPTER 5

A Parametric EWS Model of Currency Crises for East Asia

Younghoon Koo, Chang Seok Oh, Hyunsoo Joo, Seungjae Lee, and Jose Antonio Tan III

5.1 Introduction

A parametric early warning system (EWS) model attempts to estimate the probability of a financial crisis by using discrete choice econometric methods, which usually take either a probit or logit approach. Earlier studies on parametric EWS models were mostly based on annual data (see, for example, Frankel and Rose 1996). Such models could be useful in identifying causes of financial crises, but may not be suitable for real-time forecasting of crisis probabilities due to their low frequency. More recently, however, there have been heightened efforts to develop parametric EWS models using monthly data aimed at real-time forecasting. A notable example is the Developing Country Studies Division (DCSD) model of currency crises developed and being used by the International Monetary Fund (IMF).[1]

The DCSD model follows the probit approach, and was estimated from monthly data of 23 emerging economies (Berg and Pattillo 1999). The model defines a currency crisis as an episode (a month) when the weighted average of currency depreciation and reserve losses exceeds its sample mean by three standard deviations. It uses five explanatory variables to predict crisis probabilities.

---

[1] Berg, Borensztein, and Pattillo (2004) note that the DCSD model is one of two EWS models used by the IMF for producing forecasts.

The EWS model reported in this chapter follows the approach of the IMF's DCSD model, but differs from it in that the model is estimated using data of six East Asian countries. There are both costs and benefits of focusing on a smaller but more homogenous set of countries. A major cost is the possibility of losing useful information. Financial crises are rare events. Reducing the number of countries reduces the number of crisis episodes and variations of the dependent variable, making the estimates less efficient. On the other hand, limiting the sample to a set of homogenous countries could make the model more suited to the countries concerned. In any case, the EWS model reported in this chapter could complement the DCSD model. The fact that our model identified different sets of explanatory variables from that of the DCSD model provides a strong justification for a regional parametric EWS model for East Asian countries.

The EWS model in this chapter is estimated from monthly data spanning from January 1979 to December 1995. The dependent variable of the model is a dummy variable, which takes the value of 1 for all months that fall within a 24-month "crisis window" preceding each currency crisis, and 0 otherwise. The explanatory variables are selected from a pool of the 15 top economic and financial indicators that were identified by the nonparametric EWS model reported in the previous chapter. The selection involves estimating various models, each corresponding to a particular set of explanatory variables, and choosing the one, which we call the representative model, that conforms to economic theory, satisfies statistical tests, and has the highest explanatory power. The representative model contains seven explanatory variables.

Applying the representative model to 1996 and 1997 data as an out-of-sample test, the model is capable of predicting the 1997 Asian financial crisis in at least four of the five crisis-affected countries, depending on the estimation method used.

The rest of this chapter is organized as follows. Section 2 discusses the methodology for estimating discrete choice models and the criteria used for model selection. In Section 3, alternative logit and probit models are estimated, each using a particular subset of explanatory variables from the top 15 indicators identified in the nonparametric model reported in Chapter 4, and a representative model is identified. In Section 4, the predictive power of the representative model is evaluated in sample. In Section 5, the representative model is compared with the IMF's DCSD model. In Section 6, the model is tested whether it can predict the 1997 Asian financial crisis. Finally, Section 7 summarizes key results and offers concluding remarks.

5.2 A Parametric EWS Model

Discrete Choice Models Using Panel Data

A discrete choice model assumes that there is a latent variable, y^*_{it}, which in the case of panel data is defined by the regression relationship

$$y^*_{it} = \beta' x_{it} + \varepsilon_i + u_{it} \tag{5.1}$$

where x_{it} is a vector of explanatory variables, β' is a vector of corresponding parameters, ε_i is a country-specific effect, u_{it} is an independently and normally distributed disturbance term with zero mean and unit variance. The subscripts i and t stand for a country and period (a month in the present context), respectively. The latent variable y^*_{it} is unobservable, but a dummy variable, y_{it}, can be observed, where

$$\begin{aligned} y_{it} &= 1 \text{ if } y^*_{it} > 0 \\ &= 0 \text{ otherwise.} \end{aligned} \tag{5.2}$$

From equations (5.1) and (5.2), we get

$$\begin{aligned} \text{Prob}(y_{it} = 1) &= \text{Prob}(u_{it} > -\beta' x_{it}) \\ &= 1 - F(-\beta' x_{it}) \\ &= F(\beta' x_{it}) \end{aligned} \tag{5.3}$$

where $\text{Prob}(y_{it} = 1)$ is the probability of y_{it} being 1 conditional on $\beta' x_{it}$. The probit model assumes that $F(\beta' x_{it})$ is represented by the standard normal cumulative distribution function, $\Phi(\beta' x_{it})$, where

$$\Phi(\beta' x_{it}) = \frac{1}{\sqrt{2\pi}} \int_{-\infty}^{\beta' x_{it}} exp\left(-\frac{z^2}{2}\right) dz \tag{5.4}$$

where z is $\beta' x_{it}$ standardized by its mean and standard deviation.

An alternative to the probit model is the logit model, which assumes $F(\beta' x_{it})$ to be a logistic cumulative distribution function, $\Lambda(\beta' x_{it})$, given by

$$\Lambda(\beta' x_{it}) = \frac{e^{\beta' x_{it}}}{1 + e^{\beta' x_{it}}} \tag{5.5}$$

The country-specific term, ε_i, can be modeled as either fixed effects or random effects. In the fixed effects approach, the country-specific term is treated as a constant, while in the random effects model, it is considered a random variable with $\varepsilon_i \sim N(0, \sigma_i^2)$, where σ_i^2 is the variance of ε_i. The random effects approach can be used for both logit and probit models. In cases of the fixed effects representations, however, because most panel data have short time series and large cross-sectional units, unconditional maximum likelihood estimation—equivalent to the least squares dummy variable approach (LSDV)—often yields inconsistent and biased estimates.[2] While the use of conditional maximum likelihood estimation provides a way out of this problem, its application is limited to the fixed effects logit model and does not extend to the probit specification. However, the structure of the panel data used in this study, which is characterized by a long time series and few cross-sectional units, allows some exceptions. Heckman (1981) finds that the fixed effects probit model performs well as the time series is lengthened so long as the lagged dummy dependent variable is not included as an explanatory variable. Katz (2001) reaches a similar conclusion when comparing estimators of unconditional and conditional logit models using data with long time series. These suggest that, in cases where the panel data have long time series and few cross-sectional units, unconditional maximum likelihood estimation can be used for both fixed effects logit and probit models.

To determine the appropriate specification of the country-specific effect, the Hausman specification test can be used to choose between fixed and random effects. With regard to the choice between probit and logit modeling, Greene (2000) has noted that, as a general proposition, there is not much difference in results using either distribution in most applications.

Constructing the Dependent Variable

A two-step approach is used to construct the dummy dependent variable y_{it}. The first step is to identify the crisis episodes. Rules for identifying crisis episodes follow those used in the nonparametric EWS model reported in the previous chapter. A crisis episode occurs if month-on-month percentage changes in a country's nominal exchange rate against the US dollar, $\dot{ER}_{it}$, defined in local currency per US dollar, exceeds its sample mean by two standard deviations, i.e.,

$$\dot{ER}_{it} > \mu_{ER_i} + 2\delta_{ER_i} \tag{5.6}$$

where μ_{ER_i} is the sample mean of the month-on-month percentage changes in the exchange rate for country i, and δ_{ER_i} is the standard deviation of the month-on-month percentage changes in the exchange rate for country i. The second step is to construct the dependent variable y_{it}. Like the

[2] This is known as the "incidental parameters problem."

nonparametric model in the previous chapter, a 24-month crisis window is used. The dependent variable takes the value of 1 for all months that fall within the 24 months preceding each crisis episode and 0 otherwise. As a result, Prob(y_{it} = 1) in this chapter is the probability that a currency crisis occurs within 24 months.

Selection of Explanatory Variables

An explanatory variable may follow a different distribution for different countries, and this may affect model performance. To address this distributional heterogeneity, following Berg and Pattillo (1999), all the explanatory variables are expressed in terms of percentiles of country-specific distributions.

In selecting explanatory variables, various subsets of the top 15 indicators of the nonparametric model are examined as possible candidates. Selection is based on the statistical significance of individual coefficients and the pseudo R^2. As criteria, the individual coefficients must be significant at least at the 10% level.

Performance Evaluation

The parametric EWS model will produce an estimate of the probability of a currency crisis occurring within the next 24 months for each period. To determine whether a crisis signal should be issued or not, a cutoff probability, *p*, needs to be selected. A crisis signal is issued when the predicted probability for a particular month exceeds *p*. There are two possible outcomes when a crisis signal is issued. A signal is true if a crisis occurs within 24 months (the crisis window) or false if no crisis follows. By the same token, "no warning" is true should 24 months of tranquility follow or false if a crisis occurs during that period. These possible outcomes are summarized in Table 5.1 below.

Table 5.1 **Possible Outcomes of Predictions by an EWS Model**

	Crisis Occurs within 24 Months	**No Crisis Occurs within 24 Months**
Signal issued[a]	*A*	*B*
No signal issued	*C*	*D*

[a] A crisis signal is issued if the predicted probability exceeds a chosen cutoff probability. Otherwise, no crisis signal is issued.

- *A* equals the number of months in which the model issues a correct warning signal, that is, a signal is followed by a currency crisis within 24 months;
- *B* equals the number of months in which the model produces a false signal, that is, a crisis signal that is not followed by a crisis within 24 months;
- *C* equals the number of months in which the model misses a crisis, that is, no crisis signal is issued but a crisis actually occurs within 24 months; and
- *D* equals the number of months in which the model does not issue a crisis signal and no crisis occurs within 24 months.

A good EWS model should maximize *A* and *D*, and minimize *B* and *C*.

Based on the prediction outcomes in Table 5.1, five measures can be constructed to help determine the predictive power of the model:

(i) $(A+D)/(A+B+C+D)$ is the proportion of correct predictions;

(ii) $A/(A+C)$ is the proportion of precrisis months (that is, all the months falling within crisis windows) correctly called, with $1-[A/(A+C)]$ the proportion of precrisis months missed, also called Type-I errors;

(iii) $D/(B+D)$ is the proportion of tranquil months (that is, all the months outside crisis windows) correctly predicted, with $1-[D/(B+D)]$ the proportion of tranquil months wrongly classified as precrisis months, or Type-II errors;

(iv) $A/(A+B)$ is the proportion of correct warning signals, also called the conditional crisis probability, with $1-[A/(A+B)]$ the proportion of false warning signals; and

(v) $[B/(B+D)]/[A/(A+C)]$ is the ratio of the proportion of tranquil months wrongly classified as precrisis months to the proportion of precrisis months correctly predicted—commonly known as the noise-to-signal ratio (*NSR*) in the nonparametric EWS literature.

Obviously, for a given model and sample, these measures also depend on the chosen cutoff probability *p*. Lowering *p* is likely to increase the proportion of precrisis months correctly called, and, hence, lower Type-I errors, but reduce the proportion of tranquil months correctly predicted, and hence increase Type-II errors. The opposite is true when *p* is raised. Therefore, there is a trade-off between Type-I and Type-II errors in setting the cutoff probability. It is usually difficult to decide which type of error is more costly.

The predictive power of an EWS model can also be measured by counting the number of crisis episodes that the model is able to predict, i.e., the number of crisis episodes for which at least one warning signal is issued within the crisis window.

5.3 Estimation Results

The models are estimated using monthly data of six East Asian countries—Indonesia, Republic of Korea (Korea), Malaysia, Philippines, Singapore, and Thailand. The data are obtained from national sources and the *International Financial Statistics* of the IMF. The estimation period for each country depends on data availability. Starting dates vary: May 1987 for Indonesia; August 1981 for Korea; January 1979 for Malaysia, Philippines, and Thailand; and January 1991 for Singapore. All sample country data end in December 1995. A total of 11 currency crisis episodes occurred in the sample countries during these estimation periods.

Model estimation involves experimenting with alternative subsets of the explanatory variables taken from the top 15 indicators of the nonparametric EWS model. Starting with a regression model involving the full set of explanatory variables, the process eliminates variables that are statistically insignificant or have erroneous signs. For each set of explanatory variables tested, four alternative specifications are estimated—fixed effects logit, fixed effects probit, random effects logit, and random effects probit. Finally, the set of explanatory variables that yields the highest pseudo R^2 with each variable being statistically significant was selected, which we call the representative model. While it is possible that the set of explanatory variables yielding the highest pseudo R^2 will differ across the four alternative specifications, in this study, the same set turns out to have the highest pseudo R^2 for all four alternative specifications.

The representative model has seven explanatory variables:

- deviation from trend of the US dollar/local currency real exchange rate;
- deviation from trend of the US dollar/yen real exchange rate;
- ratio of current account balance to gross domestic investment (GDI);
- ratio of short-term external debt to foreign reserves;
- 12-month change of the lending-deposit rate spread;
- 12-month change in the ratio of deposits in Bank for International Settlements (BIS) banks to foreign reserves; and
- ratio of broad money (M2) to foreign reserves.

The regression results for this model are shown in Table 5.2. Most of the coefficients are statistically significant at 1%, and none is above the 10% significance level.

A real appreciation of a domestic currency from its trend increases the crisis probability. On the other hand, a positive deviation of the real US dollar/yen exchange rate from its trend reduces the chance of a crisis occurring. An accumulation of short-term external debt relative to foreign reserves increases vulnerability to currency crises. Likewise, as M2 outpaces foreign reserve accumulation, an economy may find it difficult to meet a sudden demand for foreign exchange without allowing the currency to depreciate. Foreign exchange outflows, both in current and capital accounts, contribute to an economy's vulnerability to crises, as suggested by the negative coefficient of the current account balance to GDI ratio and positive coefficient of the 12-month change in the ratio of BIS deposits to foreign reserves, the latter being a proxy for capital flight. Finally, an increase in the lending-deposit rate spread, an indicator of financial sector health, increases crisis probability.

The random effects logit and probit specifications each has a pseudo R^2 of about 39%, and for the fixed effects logit and probit models, the pseudo R^2 is about 50%. Applying the Hausman specification test to determine whether the fixed or random effects representation is more appropriate, it is found that random effects is the more appropriate representation.

5.4 Assessing In-Sample Predictive Performance

Table 5.3 reports the results of in-sample evaluation of model performance. With the average unconditional crisis probability estimated to be about 24% for the sample countries,[3] two alternative cutoff probability levels, 30% and 40%, are chosen to evaluate the predictive power of the model. The model issues a warning signal when the estimated probability exceeds the chosen cutoff level.

Table 5.3 shows that, at a cutoff probability of 30%, *NSRs* of the four alternative specifications range from 0.062 to 0.152. This means that the probability of the model issuing a true warning of an impending crisis is at least 6.6 times greater than issuing a false alarm. The probability of a crisis

[3] This means that the months falling within crisis windows of the 11 crisis episodes accounted for about 24% of the total months during the sample period.

Table 5.2 **Regression Results—Representative Model**

	Fixed Effects		Random Effects	
	Logit	**Probit**	**Logit**	**Probit**
Constant	-8.93***	-5.17***	-9.66***	-5.73***
	(-8.65)	(-9.14)	(-9.01)	(-10.35)
US$/local currency real exchange rate, deviation from trend	0.05***	0.03***	0.05***	0.03***
	(9.75)	(10.4)	(9.65)	(10.44)
Short-term external debt/foreign reserves	0.03***	0.02***	0.03***	0.02***
	(4.32)	(4.66)	(4.38)	(5.11)
Deposits in BIS banks/foreign reserves, 12-month change	0.01**	0.005**	0.01*	0.004*
	(1.98)	(1.98)	(1.85)	(1.92)
M2/foreign reserves	0.04***	0.02***	0.04***	0.02***
	(5.94)	(6.16)	(5.82)	(6.14)
Current account balance/GDI	-0.01**	-0.01*	-0.01**	-0.01**
	(-2.14)	(-1.91)	(-2.23)	(-1.99)
Lending-deposit rate spread, 12-month change	0.01***	0.01***	0.01***	0.01***
	(3.22)	(3.07)	(3.1)	(3.01)
US$/yen real exchange rate, deviation from trend	-0.02***	-0.02***	-0.02***	-0.01***
	(-6.14)	(-6.46)	(-6.06)	(-6.43)
Pseudo R2	0.500	0.504	0.386	0.391
Number of observations	949	949	949	949

BIS = Bank for International Settlements, GDI = gross domestic investment, M2 = broad money.
Note: Numbers in parentheses are z-ratios.
*** Indicates that the coefficient is significant at 1%.
** Indicates that the coefficient is significant at 5%.
* Indicates that the coefficient is significant at 10%.
Source: Authors' estimates.

Table 5.3 **In-Sample Performance Evaluation—Representative Model**

	Fixed Effects		Random Effects	
	Logit	**Probit**	**Logit**	**Probit**
Cutoff Probability of 30%				
% of observations correctly called [(*A*+*D*)/(*A*+*B*+*C*+*D*)]	86.2	86.0	85.2	85.0
% of precrisis periods correctly called [*A*/(*A*+*C*)]	80.0	80.4	48.7	47.4
% of tranquil periods correctly called [*D*/(*B*+*D*)]	88.2	87.8	96.9	97.1
Noise-to-signal ratio [[*B*/(*B*+*D*)]/[*A*/(*A*+*C*)]]	0.148	0.152	0.063	0.062
Conditional probability (%) of a crisis [*A*/(*A*+*B*)]	68.4	67.8	83.6	83.8
Number of crisis episodes predicted[a]	10	10	8	8
Cutoff Probability of 40%				
% of observations correctly called [(*A*+*D*)/(*A*+*B*+*C*+*D*)]	87.2	86.9	83.8	83.4
% of precrisis periods correctly called [*A*/(*A*+*C*)]	74.3	74.3	37.8	36.1
% of tranquil periods correctly called [*D*/(*B*+*D*)]	91.4	91.0	98.5	98.5
Noise-to-signal ratio [[*B*/(*B*+*D*)]/[*A*/(*A*+*C*)]]	0.116	0.122	0.040	0.042
Conditional probability (%) of a crisis [*A*/(*A*+*B*)]	73.4	72.5	88.8	88.3
Number of crisis episodes predicted[a]	10	10	7	7

[a] Actual number of crisis episodes in the sample is 11.
Source: Authors' estimates.

occurring within 24 months after a warning signal is issued, also called the conditional crisis probability, ranges between 67.8% and 83.8%.

On average, the representative model makes correct predictions in about 85.6% of in-sample months. The fixed effects specifications correctly predict larger proportions of precrisis months than their random effects counterparts—an average of 80% versus 48%. The fixed effects specifications are able to capture 10 of the 11 crisis episodes during the sample period by issuing at least one early warning signal, while the random effects counterparts are able to capture 8 episodes. However, the random effects specifications have lower *NSRs* compared with the fixed effects models. Also, the conditional crisis probabilities of the random effects specifications are higher. These findings suggest that the random effects specifications are able to give more reliable signals. In contrast, while fixed effects models correctly call a larger proportion of precrisis periods, they also have larger Type-II errors, that is, a higher proportion of tranquil periods misclassified as precrisis periods.

When the cutoff probability level is raised to 40%, the range of *NSRs* of the four alternative specifications lowers to 0.04–0.122, suggesting improved reliability of the model's warning signals. This is also evidenced by the range of conditional crisis probabilities, which increases to 72.5–88.8%. However, the proportion of precrisis months correctly called falls to a range of 36.1–74.3%. The model is able to issue at least one early warning signal for 7–10 of the 11 crisis episodes during the sample period. The random effects models continue to exhibit lower *NSRs* and conditional crisis probabilities compared with the fixed effects counterparts.

5.5 Comparison with the DCSD and DCSD-Type Models

To further evaluate the predictive power of the representative model, a comparison is made with the IMF's DCSD model. The DCSD model employs five explanatory variables: (i) deviation of the real US dollar/local currency exchange rate from its trend, (ii) ratio of current account balance to gross domestic product (GDP), (iii) 12-month growth of foreign reserves, (iv) 12-month growth of exports, and (v) ratio of short-term external debt to foreign reserves.[4] Two comparisons are made—the first is with the DCSD model

[4] An earlier version of the DCSD model used the ratio of M2 to foreign reserves, instead of the ratio of short-term external debt to foreign reserves.

presented in Berg and Pattillo (1999) and the second with a model estimated by employing the same set of explanatory variables as the DCSD model but using data for the six East Asian countries, which we call the "DCSD-type model."

Comparison with the DCSD Model

Berg and Pattillo (1999) present three alternative probit specifications of the DCSD model. Among the three, the one with explanatory variables entered linearly in percentiles was considered the preferred specification. This specification is taken as a comparator for our representative model. Table 5.4 shows that, at a 25% cutoff probability,[5] all four specifications of the representative model outperform the DCSD model in sample. The *NSR* of the DCSD model is higher at 0.333 compared with the range of 0.083–0.182 for the representative model. The conditional crisis probability of the DCSD model is 37%, at least 27 percentage points lower. Its proportion of precrisis months correctly called is also lower than the representative model.

Differences between the two models, however, make the above comparison problematic. First, the two models cover different time periods for in-sample evaluation. For instance, the DCSD model covers the period from January 1970 to April 1995 while the representative model uses data ranges that start later and end in December 1995. Second, the country coverage of the two models also differs. The DCSD model covers 23 countries while the representative model is much narrower, covering only 6 countries. Finally, the two models use different definitions of currency crisis episodes. The DCSD model uses the exchange market pressure index, while the representative model uses percentage changes in exchange rates.

Comparison with the DCSD-Type Model

To allow for some of these disparities, an alternative model—called the DCSD-type model—is estimated using the same set of explanatory variables as the DCSD model, but with the crisis definition and data set of the representative model. The sample period for the DCSD-type model, however, is longer than that for the representative model as more observations are available for explanatory variables. The sample period begins January 1981

[5] Berg and Pattillo (1999) also performed model evaluation at a 50% cutoff probability, and found that their model was unable to predict any crisis episodes in the out-of-sample period.

Table 5.4 **In-Sample Performance Evaluation—Representative vs. DCSD Model**

	Representative Model				
	Fixed Effects		Random Effects		DCSD Model
Cutoff Probability of 25%	**Logit**	**Probit**	**Logit**	**Probit**	**Probit**
% of observations correctly called [(*A*+*D*)/(*A*+*B*+*C*+*D*)]	84.9	84.5	85.6	85.5	78.0
% of precrisis periods correctly called [*A*/(*A*+*C*)]	83.5	83.9	55.2	53.9	48.0
% of tranquil periods correctly called [*D*/(*B*+*D*)]	85.4	84.7	95.3	95.5	84.0
Noise-to-signal ratio [[*B*/(*B*+*D*)]/[*A*/(*A*+*C*)]]	0.175	0.182	0.086	0.083	0.333
Conditional probability (%) of a crisis [*A*/(*A*+*B*)]	64.6	63.7	78.9	79.5	37.0

Source: Authors' estimates and Berg and Pattillo (1999).

for Indonesia, January 1976 for Korea, January 1974 for Malaysia, January 1977 for the Philippines, December 1985 for Singapore, and January 1975 for Thailand. It ends in December 1995 for all sample countries. There are a total of 16 currency crisis episodes in the sample. Like the representative model, four alternative specifications are estimated, with the results shown in Table 5.5.

All the coefficients have a correct sign, and are significant at either 1% or 5% level, except for the 12-month growth rate of foreign reserves, which is insignificant in all specifications. An appreciation in the real exchange rate relative to its trend or an increase in the ratio of short-term external debt to foreign reserves raises the probability of a currency crisis, while an increase in export growth, in the ratio of current account balance to GDP, or in foreign reserve growth reduces the crisis probability. The pseudo R^2s are about 15% for the two random effects specifications and 20% for the two fixed effects specifications. But the Hausman specification test suggests that the random effects specification is the more appropriate representation. A comparison of the DCSD-type model with the representative model shows that, in terms of the pseudo R^2, the representative model performs better, with the pseudo R^2 at least 18 percentage points higher.

Table 5.6 reports the results of an in-sample evaluation for the DCSD-type model. At a 30% cutoff probability, *NSRs* range from 0.372 to 0.598, substantially higher than the 0.062–0.152 range for the representative model, suggesting that the warning signals issued by the representative model are more reliable. This is also confirmed by the conditional crisis probabilities of the representative model, which are higher by about 16–44 percentage points than those of the DCSD-type model. The proportion of precrisis months correctly called varies depending on the treatment of country-specific effects. The fixed effects specifications of the representative model have higher proportions of correctly predicted precrisis periods compared with its DCSD-type counterparts, while the opposite is true for the random effects specifications. Similar observations can be made on the relative performance of the two models when the cutoff probability is raised to 40%.

Counting the number of crisis episodes for which at least one warning signal is issued, the DCSD-type model slightly outperforms the representative model when the random effects specifications are employed, and the two perform nearly the same when fixed effects specifications are used.

Table 5.5 **Regression Results—DCSD-Type Model**

	Fixed Effects		Random Effects	
	Logit	**Probit**	**Logit**	**Probit**
Constant	-2.48***	-1.41***	-2.72***	-1.41***
	(-4.78)	(-4.67)	(-6.88)	(-5.9)
US$/local currency real exchange rate, deviation from trend	0.03***	0.02***	0.03***	0.02***
	(10.75)	(11.18)	(10.86)	(11.19)
Export growth	-0.01***	-0.01***	-0.01***	-0.01***
	(-4.53)	(-4.59)	(-4.42)	(-4.67)
Current account balance/GDP	-0.01**	-0.005**	-0.01**	-0.004**
	(-2.26)	(-2.45)	(-2.46)	(-2.37)
Short-term external debt/foreign reserves	0.02***	0.01***	0.02***	0.01***
	(5.24)	(5.39)	(5.45)	(5.31)
Foreign reserve growth	-0.004	-0.002	-0.004	-0.002
	(-1.54)	(-1.39)	(-1.58)	(-1.4)
Pseudo R^2	0.203	0.207	0.146	0.147
Number of observations	1,285	1,285	1,285	1,285

GDP = gross domestic product.
Note: Numbers in parentheses are z-ratios.
*** Indicates that the coefficient is significant at 1%.
** Indicates that the coefficient is significant at 5%.
* Indicates that the coefficient is significant at 10%.
Source: Authors' estimates.

Table 5.6 **In-Sample Performance Evaluation—DCSD-Type Model**

	Fixed Effects		Random Effects	
	Logit	**Probit**	**Logit**	**Probit**
Cutoff Probability of 30%				
% of observations correctly called [(*A*+*D*)/(*A*+*B*+*C*+*D*)]	72.8	71.8	68.9	62.2
% of precrisis periods correctly called [*A*/(*A*+*C*)]	67.1	67.4	57.9	65.5
% of tranquil periods correctly called [*D*/(*B*+*D*)]	75.0	73.5	73.3	60.9
Noise-to-signal ratio [[*B*/(*B*+*D*)]/[*A*/(*A*+*C*)]]	0.372	0.393	0.462	0.598
Conditional probability (%) of a crisis [*A*/(*A*+*B*)]	51.9	50.5	46.5	40.2
Number of crisis episodes predicted[a]	15	15	14	15
Cutoff Probability of 40%				
% of observations correctly called [(*A*+*D*)/(*A*+*B*+*C*+*D*)]	74.2	73.9	75.2	70.3
% of precrisis periods correctly called [*A*/(*A*+*C*)]	54.6	55.2	41.6	53.5
% of tranquil periods correctly called [*D*/(*B*+*D*)]	82.0	81.5	88.7	77.0
Noise-to-signal ratio [[*B*/(*B*+*D*)]/[*A*/(*A*+*C*)]]	0.329	0.336	0.273	0.430
Conditional probability (%) of a crisis [*A*/(*A*+*B*)]	54.9	54.4	59.5	48.3
Number of crisis episodes predicted[a]	14	14	14	14

[a] Actual number of crisis episodes is 16.
Source: Authors' estimates.

5.6 Predicting the 1997 Asian Financial Crisis

A performance evaluation of the representative model is conducted using out-of-sample data, specifically, by extending the forecasting range until the month immediately preceding the 1997 crisis episode for each country. The crisis episode for each country is as follows: July 1997 for the Philippines and Thailand; August 1997 for Malaysia and Singapore; November 1997 for Korea; and December 1997 for Indonesia. This is to test whether the representative model is capable of predicting the onset of the 1997 Asian financial crisis. Again, two alternative cutoff probabilities of 30% and 40% are used. Table 5.7 reports the number and lead time of warning signals for each specification of the representative model.

At a 30% cutoff probability, the random effects specifications of the representative model are able to capture the 1997 crisis in all crisis-affected countries, while the fixed effect counterparts miss Indonesia. All specifications, however, are unable to predict the crisis episode in Singapore. The random effects models work well for Indonesia, Malaysia and, to a lesser extent, Thailand. They issue 21 signals with a lead time of 24 months for Indonesia, 23 signals with a lead time of 23 months for Malaysia and 16-17 signals with a lead time of 22 months for Thailand. For Korea, only 8 signals are issued with a lead time of 24 months, while for the Philippines, only 2 signals are issued with a lead time of 4 months. The fixed effects specifications perform very well in predicting the crisis episodes in Malaysia, Philippines, and Thailand. For Malaysia, warning signals are issued for the entire 24-month signaling window, while for the Philippines and Thailand, 23 warning signals are issued with a lead time of 23 and 24 months, respectively. Only 3 signals with a lead time of 3 months are issued for Korea. No signals are issued for Indonesia.

When the cutoff probability is raised to 40%, the predictive power of the representative model is reduced. The random effects specifications now miss the episode in the Philippines. The fixed effects specifications are still able to issue at least one warning signal for four of the five crisis-affected countries. The random effects specifications work well for Indonesia and Malaysia while the fixed effects counterparts perform well in predicting the crisis episodes in Malaysia, Philippines, and Thailand.

Figures 5.A.1–5.A.24 in Appendix 5.1 show crisis probabilities predicted by the representative model for both in-sample and out-of-sample periods. There are dramatic increases in predicted crisis probabilities prior to the 1997 Asian financial crisis in all five crisis-affected countries for the two random effects specifications, with the crisis probability reaching as high as

Table 5.7 **Number of Signals and Lead Time (in months) of the Representative Model within the 24 Months prior to the 1997 Currency Crisis**

	Indonesia	Korea	Malaysia	Philippines	Singapore	Thailand
Fixed Effect Logit						
Cutoff probability=30%	0 (0)	3 (3)	24 (24)	23 (23)	0 (0)	23 (24)
Cutoff probability=40%	0 (0)	1 (2)	24 (24)	21 (23)	0 (0)	22 (23)
Fixed Effect Probit						
Cutoff probability=30%	0 (0)	3 (3)	24 (24)	23 (23)	0 (0)	23 (24)
Cutoff probability=40%	0 (0)	3 (3)	24 (24)	22 (23)	0 (0)	22 (23)
Random Effects Logit						
Cutoff probability=30%	21 (24)	8 (24)	23 (23)	2 (4)	0 (0)	17 (22)
Cutoff probability=40%	20 (24)	5 (23)	21 (21)	0 (0)	0 (0)	6 (21)
Random Effects Probit						
Cutoff probability=30%	21 (24)	8 (24)	23 (23)	2 (4)	0 (0)	16 (22)
Cutoff probability=40%	19 (24)	5 (23)	21 (21)	0 (0)	0 (0)	6 (21)

Note: Figures without parentheses refer to the number of signals, while those in parentheses refer to the lead time of the first signal.
Source: Authors' estimates.

80–90% for Indonesia, Korea, and Malaysia, and at around 30–45% for the Philippines and Thailand. For the two fixed effects specifications, however, dramatic increases in the predicted crisis probabilities are only observed for Malaysia, Philippines, Thailand, and, to a much lesser extent, Korea, but not for Indonesia.

5.7 Summary and Conclusions

This chapter uses data from six East Asian countries to examine the feasibility of developing various logit and probit models as parametric early warning systems for currency crises. A representative model was identified with seven explanatory variables, including deviations from trend of the real US dollar/local currency exchange rate and of the US dollar/yen real exchange rate, ratio of short-term external debt to foreign reserves, 12-month change of the lending-deposit rate spread, 12-month change in the ratio of deposits in BIS banks to foreign reserves, ratio of current account balance to GDI, and ratio of M2 to foreign reserves. Statistical tests and regression diagnostics show that this model has the highest predictive power among possible alternatives culled from the top 15 indicators of the nonparametric EWS model.

Results of the in-sample evaluation suggest that, at a cutoff probability of 30%, the probability of the model issuing true warning signals is at least 6.6 times greater than it issuing false alarms. Once a warning signal is issued, the probability of a crisis occurring within 24 months ranges between 68% and 84%. At this cutoff level, the representative model correctly predicts between 47% and 80% of the precrisis months and between 73% and 91% of the crisis episodes during the sample period, depending on whether fixed effects or random effects specifications are used. The random effects specifications outperform the fixed effects models in terms of signal reliability. Raising the cutoff probability increases the model's conditional crisis probabilities further, hence making its warning signals more reliable, but reduces the number of precrisis months and crisis episodes correctly predicted.

When benchmarked against the DSCD and DCSD-type models, in-sample tests show that the representative model outperforms the two comparator models as the warning signals issued by the representative model are more reliable, evidenced by lower *NSRs* and higher conditional crisis probabilities. The random effects specifications of the representative model, however, have a lower proportion of correctly called precrisis periods and capture less crisis episodes compared with the DCSD-type model.

Using out-of-sample data extending to the month immediately before the 1997 crisis episodes, results show that, at a 30% cutoff probability, the random effects specifications of the representative model are able to predict the 1997 Asian crisis in all five crisis-affected countries while the fixed effects counterparts miss one country.

These results show that a discrete choice model could be an important tool for developing early warning systems for currency crises in East Asia. The fact that the representative model identifies a different set of explanatory variables, and that it outperforms the IMF's DCSD model, provides strong justification for a regional parametric EWS model. However, more work is needed to improve the predictive power of the representative model, and parametric EWS models in general, similar to the case of the nonparametric EWS models reported in the previous chapter. Many of the problems and issues outlined in Chapter 4 for nonparametric EWS models apply equally to parametric EWS models.

References

Aades, A., D. Masih, and D. Tenengauzer. 1998. A New Framework for Predicting Financial Crisis in Emerging Markets, *Economic Research*: Goldman Sachs.

Berg, Andrew, and Catherine Pattillo. 1999. Are Currency Crises Predictable? A Test. *IMF Working Papers No. 97/159.* IMF, Washington DC, November.

———. 1999. Predicting Currency Crisis: The Indicators Approach and an Alternative, *Journal of International Money and Finance* 18: 581–586.

Berg, Andrew, Eduardo Borensztein, and Catherine Pattillo. 2004. Assessing Early Warning Systems: How Have They Worked in Practice? *IMF Working Paper No. 04/52*. IMF, Washington DC, March.

Eichengreen, Barry, Andrew K. Rose, and Charles Wyplosz. 1996. Contagious Currency Crises. *NBER Working Paper No. 5681*. National Bureau of Economic Research (NBER), Cambridge, July.

Esquivel, G., and F. Larrain. 1998. Explaining Currency Crises. *Development Discussion Paper No. 666.* Harvard Institute for International Development. Harvard University, Cambridge, November.

Frankel, Jeffrey, and Andrew Rose. 1996. Currency Crashes in Emerging Markets: An Empirical Treatment, *Journal of International Economics* 41 (3/4).

Goldfajn, Ilan, and Rodrigo Valdes. 1997. Capital Flows and Twin Crises: The Role of Liquidity. *IMF Working Paper 97/87.* IMF, Washington DC.

Goldstein, Morris, Graciella L. Kaminsky, and Carmen M. Reinhart. 2000. *Assessing Financial Vulnerability: An Early Warning System for Emerging Markets.* Washington DC: Institute for International Economics.

Greene, William H. 2000. *Econometric Analysis, 4th Edition.* New Jersey: Prentice-Hall.

Hardy, Daniel, and Ceyla Pazarbasioglu. 1999. Determinants and Leading Indicators of Banking Crises: Further Evidence. *IMF Staff Papers* 46 (3).

Hawkins, J., and M. Klau. 2000. Measuring Potential Vulnerabilities in Emerging Market Economies. *BIS Working Papers 91*. Bank for International Settlements (BIS), Basle, October.

Heckman, J. 1981. The Incidental Parameters Problem and the Problem of Initial Conditions in Estimating a Discrete Time-Discrete Data Stochastic Process. In *Structural Analysis of Discrete Data with Econometric Applications*, editedby C. Manski and D. McFadden. Cambridge: MIT Press.

Herrera, Santiago, and Conrado Garcia.1999. User's Guide to an Early Warning System for Macroeconomic Vulnerability in Latin American Countries. *Policy Research Working Paper 2233*. Latin America and the Caribbean Region, Economic Policy Sector Unit, World Bank, Washington DC, November.

Kaminsky, Graciela L., Saul Lizondo, and Carmen M. Reinhart. 1998. Leading Indicators of Currency Crises. *IMF Staff Papers* 45 (1):1–48.

Katz, E. 2001. Bias in Conditional and Unconditional Fixed Effects Logit Estimation. *Political Analysis* 9 (4): 379–384.

Krolzig, Hans-Martin. 2002. *Regime Switching Models*. Lecture Notes.

Krugman, P. 1979. A Model of Balance-of-Payments Crises. *Journal of Money, Credit, and Banking* (August): 311–25.

LG Financial Research Center. 2000. *Research on Early Warning System for the Financial Markets*. LG Economic Research Institution.

Maddala, G. 1989. *Limited Dependent and Qualitative Variables in Econometrics*. Cambridge: Cambridge University Press.

Milesi-Ferretti, G., and A. Razin. 1998. Sharp Reductions in Current Account Deficits: An Empirical Analysis. *European Economic Review* 42 (3–5): 897–908.

Park, W. 2001. Prediction Models of Currency Crises in Korea. *Working Paper*. Hongik University, Korea, March.

Park, W., and K. Choi. 1998. Predicting Financial Crisis Using the Signals Approach (in Korean). *Korean Econometric Review* 9.

Rose, A. 1998. *Constructing and Using an Early Warning System: Methodology and an Application to Korea*. Mimeo.

Sachs, J., A. Tornell, and A. Velasco. 1996. Financial Crises in Emerging Markets: The Lessons of 1995. *Brookings Papers on Economics Activity* 1: 147–198.

Wu, Yih-Jiuan, Tzung-Ta Yen, and Pei-Wen Chen. 2000. *Early Warning System (EWS) for Currency Crises: An Empirical Study of Some SEACEN Countries*. The South East Asian Central Banks (SEACEN) Research and Training Centre, Kuala Lumpur, March.

APPENDIX 5.1

Currency Crisis Episodes and Predicted Crisis Probabilities

Figures 5.A.1–5.A.6 **Representative Model—Fixed Effects Logit**
Specific dates indicate crisis episodes

5.A.1 **Indonesia**

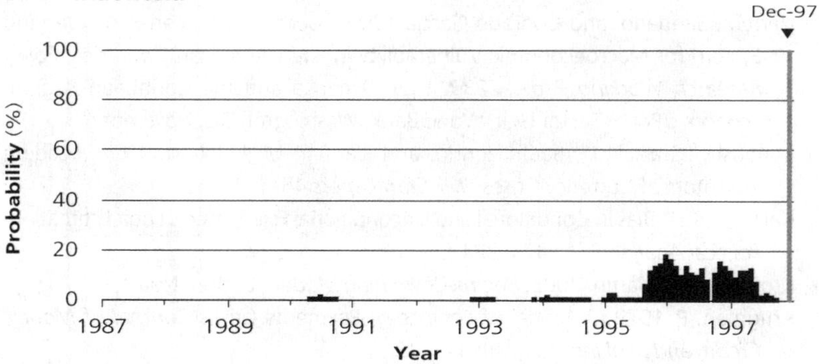

5.A.2 **Korea**

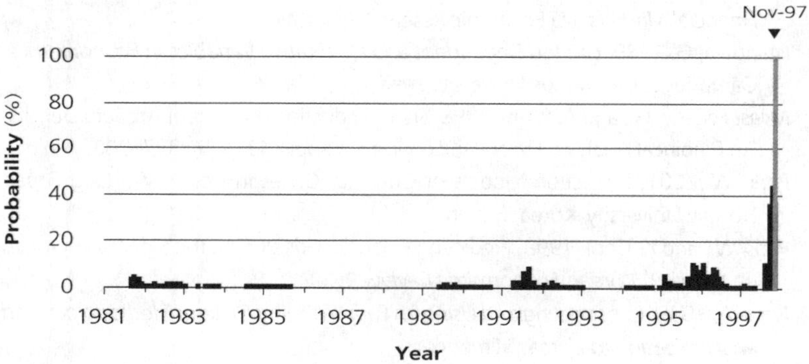

5.A.3 **Malaysia**

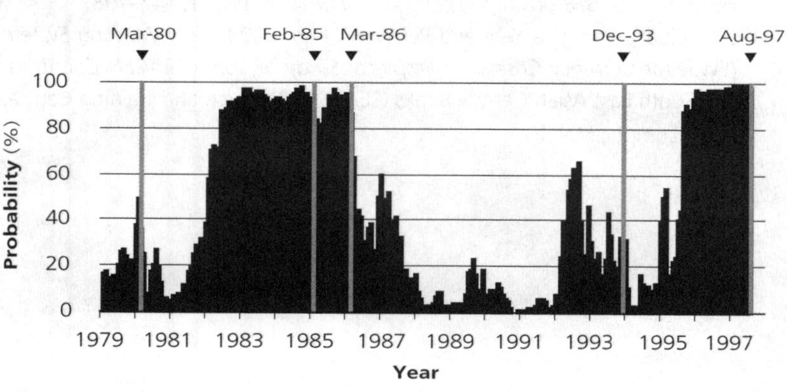

5.A.4 **Philippines**

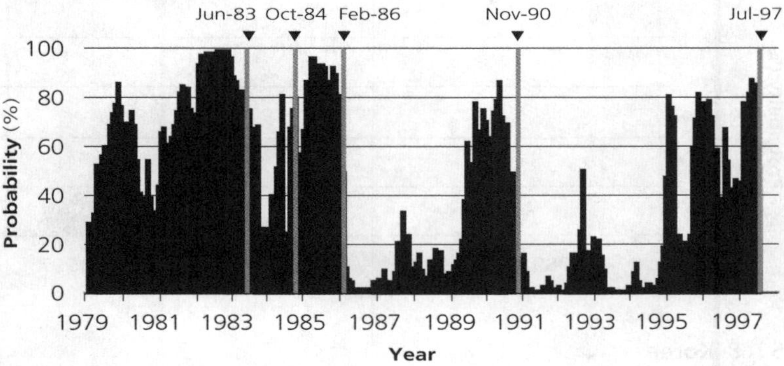

5.A.5 **Singapore**

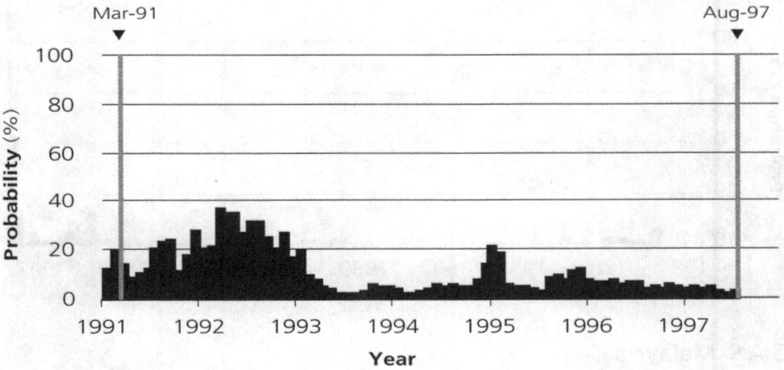

5.A.6 **Thailand**

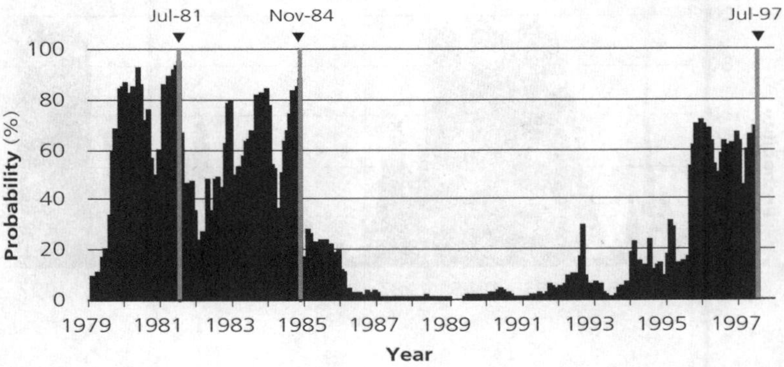

Figures 5.A.7–5.A.12 **Representative Model—Fixed Effects Probit**
Specific dates indicate crisis episodes

5.A.7 **Indonesia**

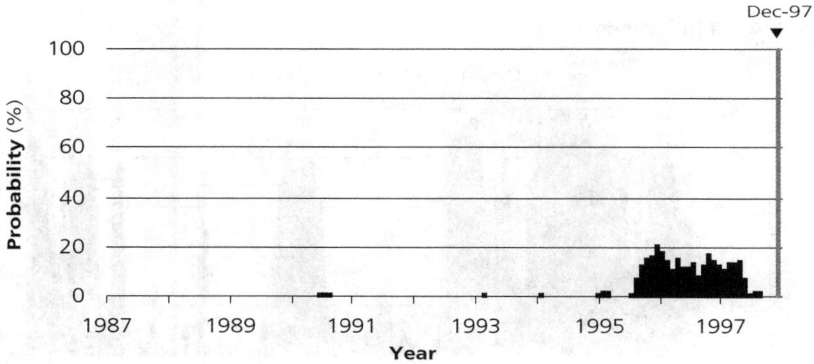

5.A.8 **Korea**

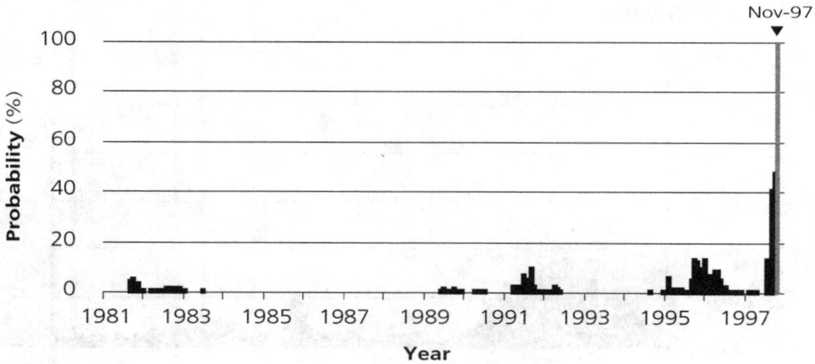

5.A.9 **Malaysia**

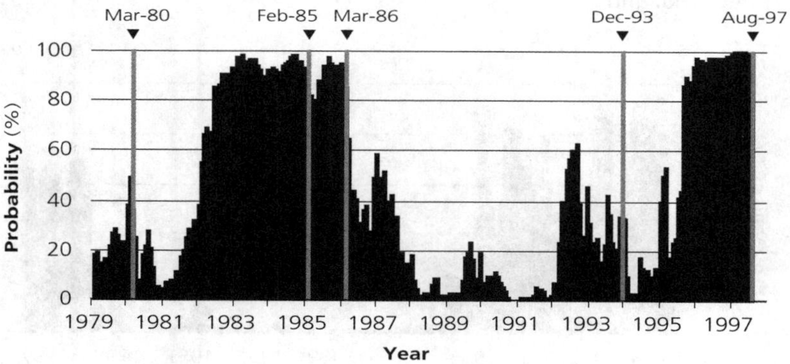

5.A.10 **Philippines**

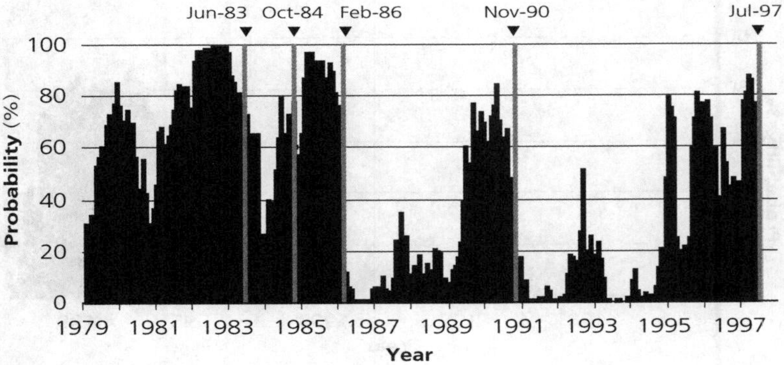

5.A.11 **Singapore**

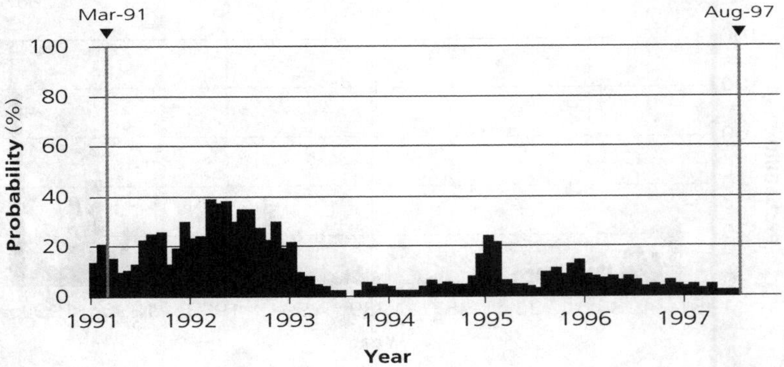

5.A.12 **Thailand**

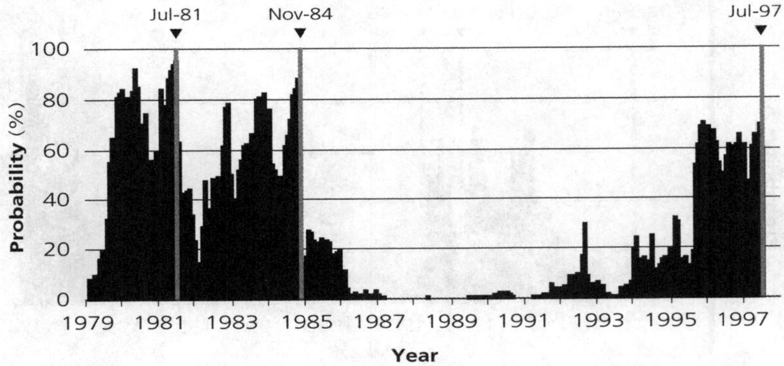

Figure 5.A.13–5.A.18 **Representative Model—Random Effects Logit**
Specific dates indicate crisis episodes

5.A.13 **Indonesia**

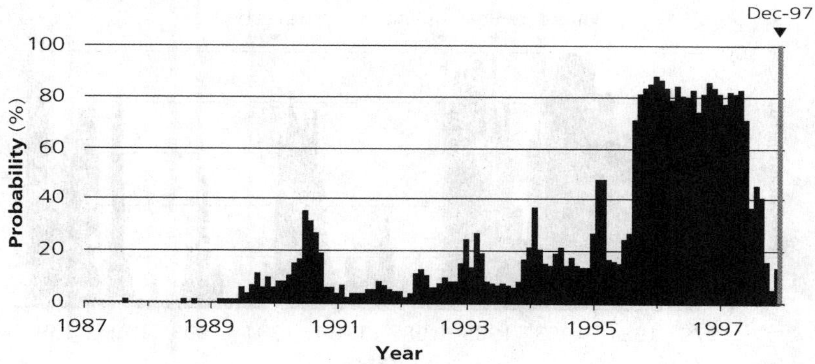

5.A.14 **Korea**

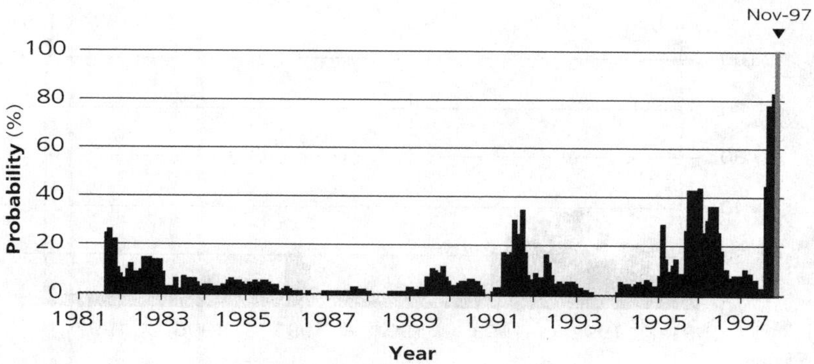

5.A.15 **Malaysia**

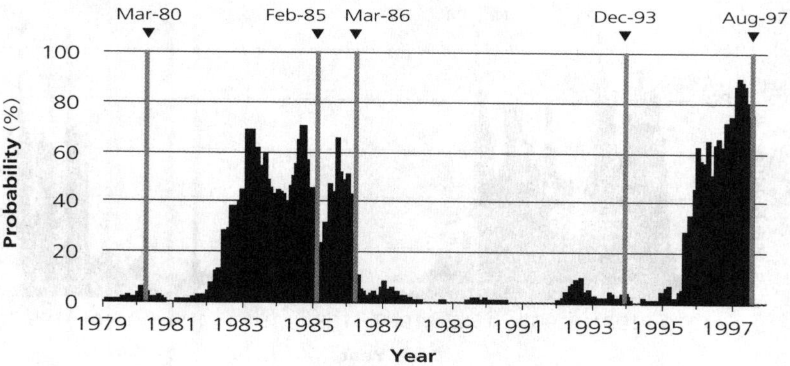

5.A.16 **Philippines**

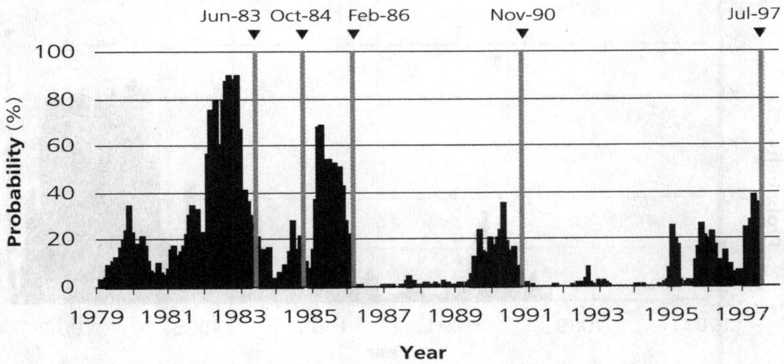

5.A.17 **Singapore**

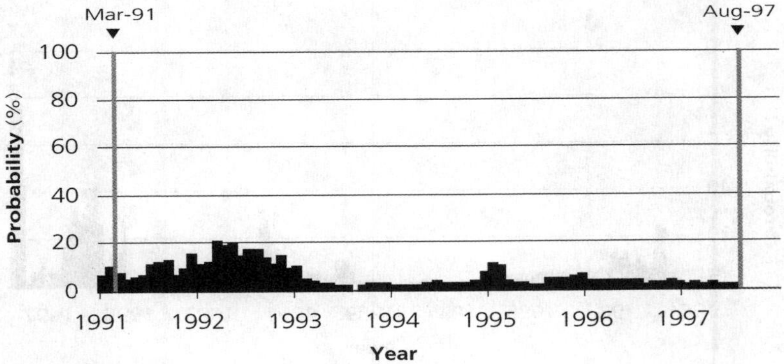

5.A.18 **Thailand**

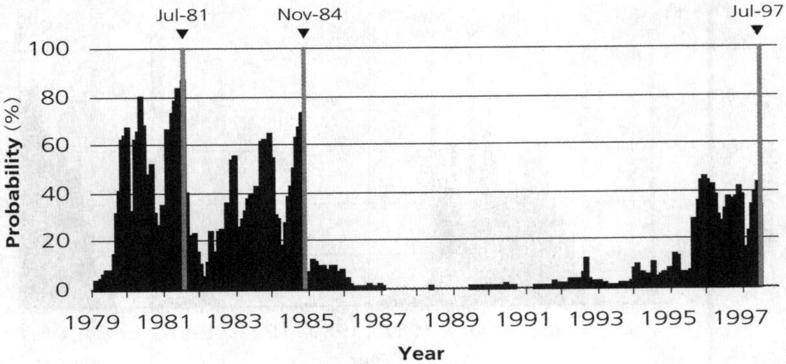

Figure 5.A.19–5.A.24 **Representative Model—Random Effects Probit**
Specific dates indicate crisis episodes

5.A.19 **Indonesia**

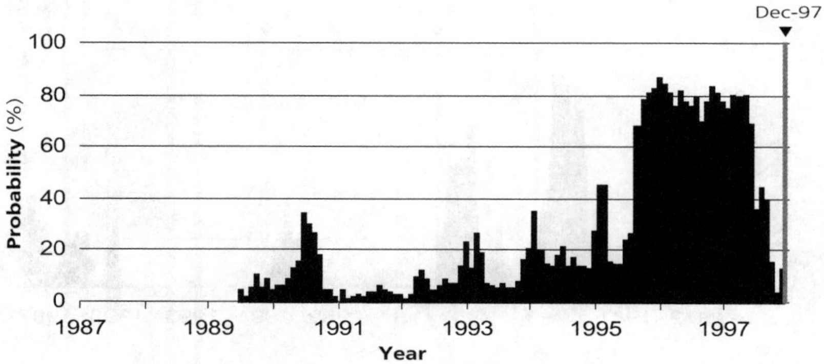

5.A.20 **Korea**

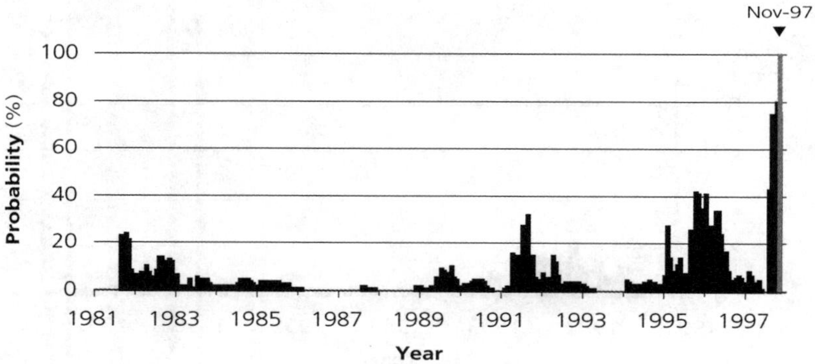

5.A.21 **Malaysia**

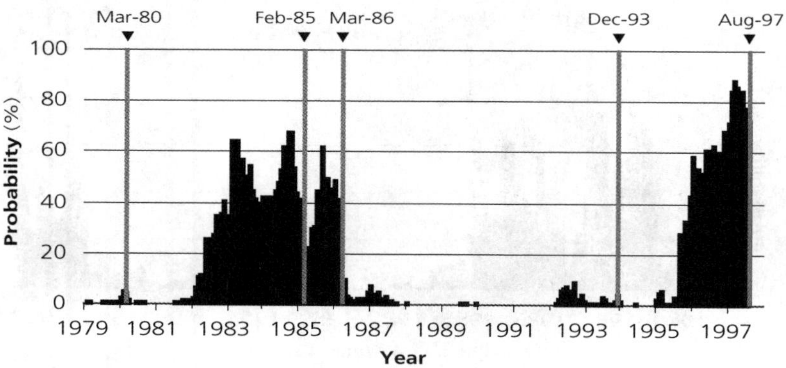

5.A.22 **Philippines**

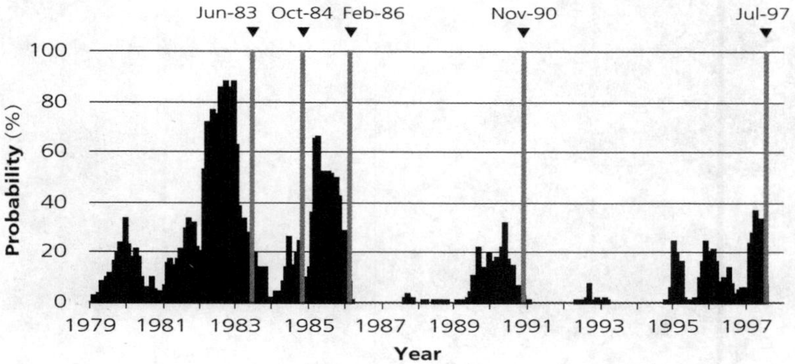

5.A.23 **Singapore**

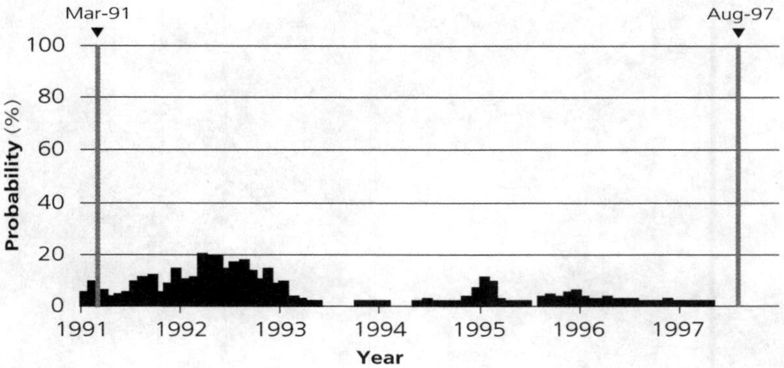

5.A.24 **Thailand**

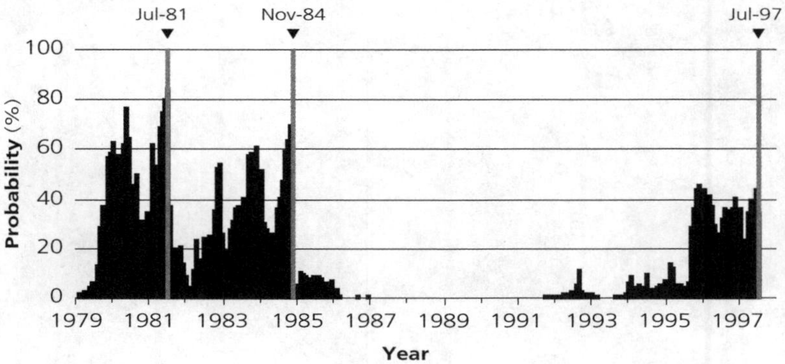